Computers, and Kids, Christian Education

How to Use
Computers in Your
Christian Education Program

By
Neil MacQueen

Contents

COMPUTERS, KIDS,
AND CHRISTIAN EDUCATION

Author: Neil MacQueen
Cover and interior design: Mike Mihelich
Cover photo: Willette Photography.

Windows™ is a trademark of Microsoft
Corporation. Macintosh® is a trademark
of Apple Computer. Pentium® is a trademark of Intel Corporation. All other
products or company names are used for
identification purposes only, and may be
trademarks of their respective owners.

ISBN 0-8066-3638-6

Manufactured in U.S.A.

1 2 3 4 5 6 7 8 9 0 1 2 3 4 5 6 7 8 9

We Are Not Drunk
Acts 2:15

At Pentecost, the Holy Spirit gave the disciples the gift of speaking in the languages of the many and diverse people gathered in Jerusalem. And the hearers were amazed: "Hey, they're speaking in languages we can understand!"

But not everyone was so amazed. "They're drunk on new wine!" said the bystanders and the naysayers.

Thank you, Lord, for Peter's gutsy response. "We're not drunk. It's only nine o'clock in the morning! A time for amazement and astonishment. A time for the young to dream dreams and the old to see visions."

The story of Pentecost has become for me the central metaphor describing why the church should be interested in exploring the use of computers in Christian education. Computers are wonderful reaching and teaching tools. They help us attract the generation of hearers milling around outside our doors. And they help us teach the Bible and share the gospel in a powerful and memorable way.

Of course, not everyone believes this. There are those who look askance at anything new or different. The idea of using computers in Christian education elicits a variety of reactions. Sometimes it comes out as a polite "we can't afford it." Some are not so polite. Like the bystanders in Peter's day, they wag their heads saying "they're drunk!"

There are people who think that those of us who advocate using computers in Christian education are drunk on technology. They wag their heads saying we have bought into the hype. Some are suspicious of anything new and unconventional.

One doesn't have to look very far to see that every age and innovation seems to have its detractors. There were those who wagged their heads at the printing press and thought the Bible read just fine in Latin. Their descendants today can't understand why kids don't just flock to their folding chairs and leaflets. They blame "kids these days" and perhaps also their parents, anyone but themselves.

Others, however, are not in retreat. They are taking seriously the gospel imperative embodied in the story of Pentecost to risk reputations and comfort zones and explore new gifts. Computers are one such gift, a learning medium that helps kids learn and want to return.

No, we're not drunk. We're just learning to speak a new language. We are learning to share the gospel in a diverse and changing world. Our task of translation never ends. And to the many gathered outside our doors, especially the children and youth of the electronic age, we can be no less astonishing and amazing in our proclamation.

Yes, computers and software are more expensive than craft sticks and tissue paper, but they also can lead to better results. And yes, it's only an hour or two a week. But...it is ONLY an hour or two a week. We must make the most of it.

What this book is about...

This book is *not* about:
➤ putting a computer in every classroom;
➤ radically changing your programs;
➤ teaching with computers instead of teachers.

This book is about putting a new tool in the hands of your teachers and students. This book is about presenting familiar and important content in a new and exciting way—through multimedia, interactive software.

This book is about the right way to bring computers into your Christian education program and the wrong way. Hundreds of churches have gone before you experimenting with these new tools. This book shares their successes and mistakes.

This book is also about my own experiences teaching with computers. I am a parent of three young children and a Presbyterian pastor specializing in Christian education. For the past seven years I have been helping kids learn with computers in Sunday school, at home, and in public school where I have volunteered as a computer dad. I have spent a great deal of time side by side with children, youth, and adults exploring the world of Christian software. Along the way, I began leading seminars, sharing teaching materials, and helping others start their own exploration with these tools. With the help of several friends, I began a "kitchen table" ministry in 1995, Sunday School Software, to provide pastors and educators with a ministry of software evaluation, lesson materials, and technical help.

My ministry has taken me across the country talking with educators and pastors about their Christian education computing experiences. We all stand on somebody's shoulders. As you read this book, you are invited to stand on the shoulders of those who have gone before you in bringing new technology to this ministry of education.

> *This book is about putting a new tool in the hands of your teachers and students.*

The Case for Computers in Christian Education

If you fly often, think about this: when was the last time you actually watched the flight attendant's entire safety demonstration? Many people, including me, routinely ignore them. On a recent trip, however, this wasn't the case. I was intently watching the demonstration. "Insert the clip into the buckle...in case of an emergency an oxygen mask will..." In the middle of the demonstration I turned around to see that everyone else was watching as if their lives depended on it! Why was everyone watching? The demonstration was being presented on video screens suspended from the ceiling of the plane!

We are multimedia-loving beings. God has created us this way and given us a special thirst for visual information and multisensory learning. Recognizing this gift, computers are exactly the kind of tool you would expect human beings to create and naturally enjoy using. Computers are no accident or aberration, and we are just beginning to explore their potential.

MULTIMEDIA LEARNING

A lot has been discovered in the past couple of decades about how the human mind learns and remembers. When multiple senses are involved, learning is a richer experience.

Multimedia Learning Is Not New

This insight is not new to Sunday school teachers. They have been employing this knowledge for decades. Our lessons have routinely included music, art, drama, memory work, and movement along with good old reading and writing. Christian educators have always used audiovisual tools to enhance teaching—fish drawn in the dirt, stained-glass windows, Bible story pictures, flannelgraph figures, filmstrips, or videos.

Scientists tell us that the brain's storage capacity has been wired (by God) mostly for visual information—nearly 80 percent of it by some accounts. Indeed, our faith story reflects such wiring. The Bible is primarily a collection of vivid stories, symbols, and images. It has only been in the last 500 years that these stories have become widely retold through text.

Jesus himself was a wonderful audiovisual teacher. As he walked the roads of Galilee, he drew his followers' attention to things they could see and then hung meaning on those images. "The kingdom of heaven is like a mustard seed that

> *Jesus himself was a wonderful audiovisual teacher.*

grows ...." "Look at the birds of the air ...." "See that fig tree ...." Even his death became a graphic symbol of indelible magnitude. His life and teachings are truths wrapped in images and compelling story.

MULTIMEDIA LEARNING IN A NEW FORM

New multimedia computer software brings the text of the Bible alive for the learner and teacher. It combines the teaching power of vivid images, music, sound, the spoken word, the written word, art, and graphics. This constellation of media is exactly the kind of information that excites the mind's learning capacity and encourages its use. Indeed, it is the combination of media around content that gives depth and dimension to the mind's capacity to comprehend and remember that content.

Benefits of Multimedia Software

The computer has an additional educational benefit of its own: interactivity. By interactivity I mean the ability to control pace and selection of content, and the ability to prompt student input and give feedback.

With the mouse, keyboard, and good educational software, spectators become participants. Learners deal with content at their own pace. Inquisitive kids can explore subjects in more depth. Students can be tested for comprehension. They can express themselves and their understanding of content.

And let us not forget that computers are fun to use! In a time when competition for our kids' attendance and attention is fierce, we cannot afford to ignore a powerful teaching and attracting tool like the computer.

What Computers Cannot Do

I never met a computer or piece of software that could replace a teacher. Beat teachers in chess, yes, but replace them, no. One of the biggest surprises in store for you and your teachers as you begin to use software is what it is like teaching with computers. Some teachers imagine that they will be relegated to "fifth wheel" status. Nothing could be further from the truth. Software is a teacher's medium because it is about content. It takes a living, breathing, caring person of faith to bring that content to life for a community of learners and help them apply it to their daily lives.

I have also never met a piece of software that could meet the entire needs of a lesson plan. There is still an important place for Bible study in other media, worship, prayer, community building, and service. In Chapters 6 and 7, you'll hear this loud and clear.

Finally, I have never met a piece of educational software that cut off discussion among teacher and learners. It is a popular misconception that healthy discussion stops when the computing begins. And it is simply not true.

I never met a computer or piece of software that could replace a teacher.

GETTING STARTED

What Happened to Us

When we began using computers in our Sunday school back in 1990, our kids went nuts. Attendance grew, Bible knowledge increased, and visitors became members (usually under pressure from their children). We quickly went from using two donated computers to having five computers in our Bible Computer Lab. Looking back on this now, what amazes me most is that we saw these results using mediocre software that doesn't even compare to today's great software.

The reaction of our parents was marvelous. They, too, wandered wide-eyed into the world of multimedia learning. Rather than rushing their kids out of our computer lab, parents stayed in the classroom to talk with teachers and sit with their children at the computer.

Our teachers were also impressed with the results. They discovered that computers dramatically improved Bible literacy and their students' attitudes. We knew that repetition and refreshment were the cornerstone of Bible literacy, but had always found this to be an elusive goal. We found that our computers made making and taking quizzes easy, repeatable, measurable, and fun.

And, guess what—our kids thought our Bible Computer Lab was very cool. When it was their turn to be in there, you could bet moms and dads got an early wake-up call. And like the crowd at Pentecost, they were pretty amazed to hear the Bible in a language that was pleasing and understandable to them. Our problems changed from how to get them to come to how to get them to leave.

It Could Happen to You

The good news is that many other churches are sharing the same story and results. A few of those stories are recounted in Chapter 9.

But there's even more good news! Pastors and educators around the country have been surprised by the ease in getting started with computers and the support they are receiving from their congregations. Many tell stories like this one:

An older leader in my congregation approached me one night after a meeting and said, "Neil, if we would have had something like this when my kids were around, maybe they would have liked coming to church. As it is, they don't want to come back and they're not bringing my grandkids. Anything you can do to change that for parents today is all right by me." Let me tell you right now that some of your older members are going to be your best supporters. They will be thrilled to see happy students and the emphasis on Bible literacy.

Kids who are eager to learn make for happy and supportive parents. And if your experience is like many, visitors out shopping for churches will become members, saying how impressed they are with the innovation and commitment.

I know this sounds like a late-night infomercial. Christian educators all too often hear about "the next great thing" and "new and improved." So my suggestion is this: come and see for yourself. Grab one or two of the programs recommended in this book, load them on a computer, and invite a few kids to join you. Their reaction and your own will tell you a lot of what you need to know.

Kids who are eager to learn make for happy and supportive parents.

Chapter 2

Getting Started Is Easier Than You Think

IT'S A GOOD TIME TO START

A number of factors are combining in our world right now to make getting started with computers in your Christian education program easier than you might think:

➢ There is an increasingly large amount of used computer equipment floating around that may be donated to you free of charge or sold to you for a low price. This is a new opportunity that didn't exist several years ago.

➢ The costs of new and used computers have dramatically decreased.

➢ Computers are becoming an accepted piece of educational equipment in homes, workplaces of all kinds, public schools, and libraries.

➢ Computer literacy is often more prevalent in congregations than Bible literacy. Most churches have plenty of people who know how to use these tools. Most churches also have a "techie"—a person who understands computers and how to make them work—among their members. You may have several!

➢ The Christian software industry is growing and producing a terrific variety and depth of software at reasonable prices.

➢ Many church staff persons are pleasantly surprised by their members' reactions to the idea of using computers and their willingness to contribute money and resources. Many people in our churches have been waiting for something truly innovative that will help attract the younger generation to Christian education.

One of the biggest problems faced by some churches is trying to decide which of the computers they've had donated to keep or pitch! Used computers are a dime a dozen in many communities and congregations, and it's only going to get worse (or better, depending on how you look at it). Some of it can be great to start with. The kind of hardware worth starting with changes as the technology moves forward. Many businesses and serious computer users replace their computers about every two years. Whatever was popular two years ago is probably available for donation now. Some of it can be upgraded to suit your needs.

WHERE TO START

You should strive to begin your exploration into computer-assisted learning with CD-capable computers. This will allow you to take advantage of a wider selection of software and some of the best. By CD-capable I mean a 586

Computer literacy is often more prevalent in congregations than Bible literacy.

generation PC (commonly referred to as a "Pentium") or a Power Macintosh. Read Chapter 4 for more details. CD-capable computers are just now coming into the donation market, in addition to being relatively inexpensive to purchase new.

If you cannot get started with a CD-capable computer and can only get started with an older computer, make sure it is at least a 486 IBM-compatible personal computer with Windows 3.1. This will allow you to run some of the older, nice software long enough to get a feel for this technology. A computer that is not CD-capable and can only use 3.5" diskette-based software will limit your software selection and quality. It can be a start but isn't where you want to be. Most of the best software is on CD-ROM.

Due to the general availability of 486 personal computers, I do not recommend getting started with 386's or 286's. Older Macintoshes are also not recommended as there was very little Christian software produced for them. Read Chapter 4 on hardware for more information.

START-UP RECOMMENDATIONS

The most important start-up recommendation is this: start slow, start small, and start with an experiment. I have met quite a few educators and pastors who were able to jump in to teaching with computers on a large scale because of a large donation and a lot of enthusiasm. Most of them end up crashing and burning because their teachers feel overwhelmed and under-prepared. Starting small as an experiment gives your teachers the time to get acquainted with the software and hardware. Most importantly, it allows them to get a feel for what it means to teach with computers and kids in the same classroom.

This recommendation applies equally to the teachers who are computer novices and teachers who are skilled with computers. Experienced teachers may be able to get the hardware all turned on and the software loaded, but that doesn't guarantee they can teach effectively with computers. This also applies to those who may have taught using computers in a public school setting. I can't tell you the number of times I've heard experienced public school educators remark how different it is to teach with computers in the church setting.

The most important start-up recommendation is this: start slow, start small, and start with an experiment.

Creating an Experiment

➢ Find a CD-capable computer. This may be an office computer, a staff computer, or one brought from home. If you can, start with two computers. This will give your teachers a feel for what it is like to manage a future lab setting with two different groups of students working on software at the same time.

➢ Find two teachers who aren't afraid of computers. Ask them to commit to five to eight weeks of Sunday morning experimentation.

➢ Select your first teachers very carefully for your experiment. Techies (remember—those people in your church who are skilled in using computers) will be helpful getting the hardware together and running, but they may not know how to teach kids, let alone teach them with a computer. In general, you will want to recruit real teachers. By "real" I mean the kind of teacher who understands the age level of the learners and is experienced in planning and leading a class session. These folks don't need a manual to know how to share their faith or to know what to say. They can spot what's important to teach from a mile away and know what to do with it. Computing is a skill. Teaching is an art. Find artists.

➢ Enlist four to six third or fourth graders to form your learner group. Ask for their commitment of time and attention. This age of learner is easiest to work with in the experiment stage because they can read, probably have some computer skills, and haven't yet entered the changes of adolescence that can challenge learner-teacher relationships.

➢ Select two or three pieces of software for your experiment. (See Chapter 3 for suggestions.) Look for variety instead of trying to match software to the scope and sequence of your Sunday school curriculum at this point. Have your teachers create two or three approaches to each program to experiment with over the weeks.

➢ Find a place for your experiment to take place. A nice cozy atmosphere will work better than a large classroom.

➢ Keep in touch with the experiment teachers and get some class time teaching with computers yourself if you are not one of the teachers. After your experiment, sit down with your teachers to create a plan for future use.

Explore the Possibilities

Teaching with computers isn't rocket science, it is just different. Your experiment will help you and your teachers explore the opportunities and limitations of this medium. After your experiment, read this book again for a second time. New insights will pop out at you. Dream together about how to weave computer time into your Sunday school curriculum and schedule.

After your period of exploration, expand slowly. You don't want to let the computer lab and the enthusiasm of your kids overwhelm your teachers' ability to manage their new tasks.

I have reviewed this "start slow" recommendation time and again with quite a few churches who have taken this advice and those who have not taken this advice. All agree: it is "getting started" gospel. Start with an experiment. Go slow. Let your experience, your intuition as teachers, and the collective wisdom of this book inform your plans.

WHAT'S SO DIFFERENT ABOUT TEACHING WITH COMPUTERS?

Most of the teachers in your church have never taught with software and computers. The presence of a monitor, mouse, and attractive software moves the teacher off the center stage and into a role similar to teaching with art or videos. In this setting the teacher is no longer the "sage on the stage" but the "guide by the side." This means helping learners explore, create, and ponder together using a new kind of Christian education content provider—the computer. Some

In this setting the teacher is no longer the "sage on the stage" but the "guide by the side."

teachers find this a liberating and fun way to teach. Others find it threatening at first. They can tend to stand back and let the kids just "have at it" on the computers. This is where training, preparation, and appropriate lesson materials come in handy. See Chapters 6 and 7 for more information.

Your kids will be different too. They'll be excited and will need time to adjust, just like their teachers. Early on, their excitement will border on chaos, especially if an untrained teacher lets them "joyride" through the software. In many public schools, the kids do not get much computer time, or their time is limited to certain kinds of software. Computer time at church may be an exciting treat for them. Establishing good habits and classroom structure is extremely important.

Teaching with computers, as you would expect, is more dependent on equipment. With a video, it doesn't matter much if you add a couple of kids to the class. With computers, the teacher-learner-computer ratios are critical to your success. The last thing you want to do is invest a lot of time and spend a lot of money, only to have your vision become a blur because there are too many kids with too few computers and guides.

Another thing that makes computing so different from other Christian education settings is that Christian education leaders will be trying to explain the "why" to other church leaders and decision makers who have never seen the "what." Most people have never seen good educational software, let alone good Christian multimedia software. Showing them what is available will help you explain why you want to use this medium. When your church council sees a demonstration of a top-notch software program—such as King David walking out on the screen in Pathways through Jerusalem, introducing himself, and inviting them on a tour of his holy city, they will want to go along.

All of these issues are discussed in this book. Most of them will become apparent and easily dealt with by educators who go into their experiments slowly and with their eyes open.

God has wired us for multimedia learning. It is time for our classrooms to take better advantage of this gift with the new tools we have. Kids, computers, and education are a great match. Computers are not only great educational tools, but have the ability to attract and motivate learning as well. The public schools and Christian schools know it. Families with good educational software know it. It's time for Christian education to experience it, too. We can't afford to ignore or bore another generation into membership oblivion.

With computers, the teacher-learner-computer ratios are critical to your success.

Chapter 3

Selecting Software

The Christian software market is a relatively new market and rather poorly publicized. So, before we get any further, let me tell you about some of the neat software out there. Knowing what is available will also help you understand some of the recommendations in upcoming chapters.

The following list is not only a selection of my personal favorites, they are some of the most widely used programs in churches today. This list is also representative of different types of software. It is not a comprehensive listing. For the latest in software and recommendations, consult with the Christian software sources that follow the list. You can also contact software manufacturers directly. Their phone numbers are listed in Appendix B.

The theological perspective in the following software titles could be described as mainstream. I have found this is true of most of the Christian software market. The developers strive to hit the broad side of the theological barn in order to market and sell their products. These recommendations fall in the middle of the broad side of the barn.

FAVORITE PROGRAMS

Note: The following titles are in alphabetical order. Find this software by checking with your local Christian bookstore, denominational publisher, or the manufacturer or distributor listed at the end of each description. Phone numbers are in Appendix B. A word of caution: The manufacturers of some older software are discontinuing production of some programs or no longer making them available on 3.5" diskettes. Depending on the manufacturer, a recommended older program may no longer be available on diskette or at all.

The Amazing Bible Expedition

Sixty-two Bible stories presented in an easy-to-read format for older children. The stories read aloud, too. Covers Genesis to Revelation. Over a dozen "tell me more" icons with each story offer students an opportunity to explore more related information. Includes an expedition game through the database of stories and short video clips. A nice tool to use in combination with other programs, such as *Bible Atlas*, or *A Walk in the Footsteps of Jesus*, a CD-ROM that runs on both Windows and Macintosh. Age 7 to 13. Baker Book House.

Bible Builders

Here's a veteran personal computer (PC) program for older computers. Students select level of difficulty and then play a trivia game covering general Bible knowledge. Right answers are rewarded with a piece of a scripture puzzle. Fun game graphics. The best set of trivia questions available among programs where you can't change the content. Available only in 3.5" and CD format for DOS and Windows. For a 386 or higher, with sound card and mouse. Age 7 to adult. Bridgestone Multimedia.

Bible Grand Slam

Bible Baseball is back, and it's now a computer game. Players can select single, double, triple, or home run questions. Play against the computer or each other. Most importantly: it comes with a question editor! Windows 386 or 486 only with a CD (players run too fast on a 586) with a sound card. Age 8 to adult. Bible Games Co.

Bible Puzzle Pro

Here's a neat and easy teacher or student tool to create all sorts of Bible "pencil puzzles," including word searches and cryptograms. Input your words or verses into the program and it prints out a puzzle for home or class use. Windows 95 only, 8 megabytes of RAM required. Bob Thompson Inc. Available only through Sunday School Software.

Journey to the Promised Land

A Bible quiz program for up to four people or teams. Students race across the Sinai on the strength of their answers to multiple choice questions. First one to reach Jericho gets to watch the walls come tumbling down. Ark Multimedia Inc.'s version comes with 1,000 trivia questions. You may want to edit their questions or write your own. You can create and edit your own questions for the game by looking at the question file and sleuthing out the file code, or you can use a little program Sunday School Software wrote called *Launchpad*. It makes *Journey to the Promised Land* a usable tool. A perfect example of an older program kids still love to use. DOS, 286 or higher. Age 7 to adult. Ark Multimedia.

Kid's Interactive Bible CDs

Each of the eight CDs in this series introduce a major character of the Bible, including Moses, David, Jesus, Paul, Ruth, and Jonah. Each CD contains an animated retelling of a story from the Bible hero's life. They also contain more than 20 chapters of Scripture to read, hear, and study using the *Kid's Application Bible* study notes with the text. There's also a theater of animated Bible cartoon clips, a quiz show about the content, and a game room on each CD. Runs on both PC and Macintosh. At least 8 megabytes of RAM. Age 5 to 11. New Kids Media and Tyndale.

Bible Baseball is back, and it's now a computer game.

Kidworks Deluxe CD

A popular creative writing and illustrating program. Allows children to create their own multimedia "illustrated talking Bible storybooks" or presentations on virtually any subject. Students type in text, illustrate book pages, add special effects, and play them back. Very kid-friendly. Consider this a "must have" for any Bible Computer Lab. A CD that runs on both PC and Macintosh. 8 megabytes of RAM minimum. Age 6 to 13. Davidson Software.

Pathways through Jerusalem

An interactive multimedia journey through Jerusalem's religious, political, and archaeological history featuring King David, King Herod, and Sultan Suleiman, among other "tour guides." Information is creatively presented about Jewish, Muslim, and Christian sites, history, beliefs, and practices. King David takes you on a tour related to his life and times including a wonderful segment about the Temple. King Herod tells about his building campaign and how he dealt with the Romans leading up to the time of Jesus. Raphael takes you on a tour of Christ's last week in Jerusalem. Dirk tells about Muslim and Christian conflicts through the story of the Crusades. Weeks of great lesson material here for kids and adults. Two CDs run on PC or Macintosh. Minimum 16 megabytes of RAM recommended. Age 10 to adult. From Softkey. Available only through Sunday School Software.

PC Bible Atlas and Quickverse

There are many research Bibles available for the computer. I like Parsons Technology products because they are easy for kids to use. Their theological content is ecumenical and easy to read. *Bible Atlas* is an onscreen atlas of Bible lands with individual maps for Bible stories. Students point and click at map locations to reveal hidden information about the story. Worksheets (of your own design) can guide students across the landscape in search of information. *Quickverse* is the entire searchable Bible on your computer with built-in concordance and topical search features. Click on the Exodus map in *Bible Atlas*, click on the scripture reference in the map and *Quickverse* takes you there. Windows only. 386 or higher, 4 megabytes of RAM minimum. Age 8 to adult. Parsons Technology.

The Play and Learn Bible CD

A collection of 50 multimedia Bible stories for preschoolers written by Gilbert Beers, a terrific children's author. The stories have a "read to me" feature and fun click-point animations on each page. The CD also includes story pages to color using a paint program, puzzles, and a Bible songs sing-along. There are a couple of early reader Bible programs on the market, but none as content-rich and varied as *Play and Learn*. Runs on both PC and Macintosh. 8 megabytes of RAM minimum. Age 4 to 8. Chariot Victor.

> *I have learned not to pay much attention to who distributes or produces the program. It's important to judge software only by what's in the program itself.*

Star Chasers

An interactive multimedia adventure following three young people who magically enter the story of the first Christmas, meet the Wise Men and shepherds, and search for the baby Jesus. Along the way they learn the meaning of Christmas and even meet the prophetess Anna.

Beautifully illustrated. Several extras, including a 3-D "fractal flyover" segment on Herod's Temple. A CD-ROM for PC and Macintosh. 16 megabytes of RAM minimum. Age 8 to 13. Starborn Inc.

A Walk in the Footsteps of Jesus

A "virtual tour" of the places Jesus walked as they appear today. Students view 360-degree "photobubbles" of places such as the Sea of Galilee, Capernaum, Golgotha, Bethany, and Nazareth. These amazing pictures also include audio hot spots to click on and hear about the location and related Scripture. A good example of how the magic of multimedia brings alive for children and youth what would otherwise have been an uninteresting slide show. The CD runs on both PC and Macintosh. 8 megabytes of RAM minimum. Age 10 to adult. Parsons Technology.

Wordy

A Bible verse memory game that teaches and tests student recall of selected Scriptures. Includes an editor so you or the kids can input your own verses. It is time to take memory verses seriously again. Wordy lets your kids have fun doing it! DOS, 386 or higher. Age 8 to adult. Rue Publishing.

Other Favorites

I also like *Disciples' Diary* (Nelson), *Captain Bible* (Bridgestone), *Sunday School Tutor and Testmaker* (Sunday School Software), *Bibleland.com* (Baker), *Bookie Bookworm Bible Series* (Zondervan), *Giants of the Faith* (Back to the Bible), *Compton's Interactive Bible*, and *Super 3-D Noah* and *Exodus* for PC (two games from Wisdom Tree). By the time you read this, there will surely be a number of "new favorites."

Please note that my favorable review of one program from a developer does not mean I would recommend the rest of their software or other products, or their general ministry. I have learned not to pay much attention to who distributes or produces the program. Usually, the company that owns the distribution rights to the program didn't make it anyway. It's important to judge software only by what's in the program itself.

Also, my favorable review of a program doesn't necessarily mean that you will have great success with it. That will depend on your teachers, your learners, your setup, and your lesson materials.

System Requirement Information

In general, I recommend that you run all CD-ROM software on a computer with a minimum of 16 megabytes of RAM. The CD drive speed for these programs should be a 4 speed or better, preferably 8 or 12. Your processor speed should be a minimum of 66 MHz. New software will undoubtedly require faster speeds. See Chapter 4 for hardware information and Chapter 10 for a review of computer basics, if you need it.

FIRST SELECTIONS

Starting with a CD-capable computer allows you to explore the best software first. It also lets you see the future, even though you may have to start your lab with older equipment. You cannot go wrong taking a look at *Pathways through Jerusalem*, exploring *Kidworks Deluxe*, getting a multimedia Bible like *The Amazing Bible Expedition*, and seeing how happy kids are to review previous material with *Journey to the Promised Land*. If you want to add a few more to the list, get a copy of *Bible Atlas* and one of the "Life of" series CDs.

If you can only begin your experiment with an older 386 or 486 with Windows 3.1 and no CD-ROM, take a look at *Journey to the Promised Land, Bible Builders,* and *Bible Atlas.* There is virtually no Christian software for older Macintoshes. It is recommended that you have one copy of each program you want to use for each computer in your computer lab. Later, this chapter will make the reason for this recommendation more clear.

> *Starting with a CD-capable computer allows you to explore the best software first.*

CHRISTIAN SOFTWARE SOURCES

The following information is here to help you become a savvy Christian software consumer. Over the years I have purchased a lot of software for my church and previewed a lot of it through my ministry. I've had the opportunity to become personally acquainted with many of the software producers and distributors, their practices and points of view. There are many wonderful people who deserve our thanks and support. The Christian software industry is, however, a business, and sometimes the industry goals and practices are not compatible with those of the resource purchaser.

Christian Publishers

There are a number of sources for Christian software, including independent Christian resource producers, distributors, and denominational publishing houses. If at all possible, talk with someone in these organizations who has actually used the piece of software you are interested in purchasing.

Catalogs

Catalogs are great places to spot software, but they should not be used as your sole source of information and recommendation. Sometimes, those making decisions about what to put in the catalog may not have previewed the software. Exercise caution when catalog shopping, and ask about the return policy.

Christian Bookstores

Many Christian bookstores sell software. Be advised that in my experience most bookstore buyers rely on the manufacturer's sales literature in making their selections. Find a bookstore with a staff person who has working knowledge of the software being sold. Ask to preview the program. Find out if they will allow you to return opened software.

Secular Software Stores

Secular software stores sometimes carry religious software. In my experience, however, they rarely carry the better titles or carry them for very long. Browsing these retail shelves has also revealed a new trend—old software being repackaged as new by obscure software distributors. Sometimes distributors purchase a bulk quantity of a decent program or well-known title and then bundle it with a group of inferior resources, selling the package at a price point that is enticing. You may find a bargain this way, but be sure to preview the entire bundle, discarding the software that is not appropriate for your use.

Magazine Ads

Software ads in Christian magazines are another source of information. As with any advertising, though, some perfectly awful programs can look great in the ad copy. Occasionally you may see an advertisement from a Christian computer hardware company that sells software, or a church administration software company that has several titles for children and youth. To check these out, ask to speak with someone in the organization who has used the software.

Christian Computing Magazines

Computer trade magazines are another source of information about software. *Christian Computing* magazine is the biggest, followed by *Computing Today,* and *Church Bytes.* I read all three and have written for all three. In my experience, these magazines tend to want uncritical reviews. Two of the three magazines have an editorial policy not to print bad reviews. Their reviews are usually based on the concept of home use, which can be quite different than using the program in a classroom setting. Macintosh users will appreciate the *Christian MacIntosh Users Group* magazine.

The Internet

The Internet is another source for information about software. Once again, however, be prepared for advertising rather than objective reviews. The Internet also is home to some offbeat, theologically intense, and poorly produced software. Some of it is called shareware. With shareware, you download the program to your computer over the phone line and send in a donation or fee if you like it. Shareware Christian software is typically less developed and less expensive. It may be slightly older software from a developer who isn't working in this arena full-time. If you're using really old equipment (286's and 386's), you might find two or three worthwhile programs among quite a few not-so-worthwhile programs. Try Goshen.net and Christianitynet.net for your search.

Purchasing by Name Recognition

Can you purchase software based on the publisher's name on the box? Sometimes. Be aware that the name on the box isn't always the name of the program's creator. It may be just the distributor. Certainly, if software from one publisher has worked well for you, that's a starting place in looking for new titles.

Independent Ministries

There are a couple of independent Christian companies and ministries that catalog and sell software. My ministry, Sunday School Software, is one of them. Without question, you should determine the ministry's review methodology, selection criteria, and theological point of view. Some are selective, others sell whatever. Some specialize in reference Bibles, others specialize in Christian education or church administration software. Get to know who you are dealing with. Insist on a return policy.

TYPES OF SOFTWARE

Available Christian software varies widely in terms of content, interactivity, style of presentation, age-appropriateness, and level of difficulty. There are also different categories of software. In general, you'll want to select programs from each category for your church.

1. Bible research tools (for example, *The Amazing Bible Expedition* and *Bible Atlas*).

2. Interactive multimedia topical presentations (for example, *Pathways through Jerusalem, A Walk in the Footsteps*).

3. Multimedia Bible stories (for example, *Star Chasers, Life of Jesus*)

4. Games (for example, *Exodus, Super 3-D Noah*).

5. Quiz-making and presentation tools (for example, *Kidworks, Journey to the Promised Land, Bible Builders*).

Bible Research Tools

Bible research software includes tools such as concordances, Bible atlases, commentaries, or Bible dictionaries. They are important tools to learn to use, but their presentation is usually less entertaining than programs from the other categories. These programs are best used in conjunction with other software and learning activities.

Interactive Multimedia Topical Presentations

Topical presentation programs, such as *Pathways through Jerusalem*, are usually found only on CD-ROM and typically have extensive content delivered by creative presentations. With these programs, the teacher usually explores the software right along with the students.

> *Available Christian software varies widely in terms of content, interactivity, style of presentation, age-appropriateness, and level of difficulty.*

Multimedia Bible Stories

Multimedia Bible story programs also are usually found only on CD-ROM. These programs typically retell a Bible story through animation, video, and onscreen activities.

Games

Bible games come in a variety of different formats, and are available on CD-ROM and diskette. They mix game play with varying degrees of instructional content and are best used in conjunction with other software. They also make great end-of-class activities.

Quiz-Making and Creative Tools

I am particularly fond of software for creating quizzes. Such software gives your teachers the ability to quiz, refresh, and reinforce lesson content. Creative tools, such as *Kidworks*, allow teachers and learners to create presentations using typing or drawing programs. Some of these tools are complex and may take more time for teachers and learners to master, but they pay off handsomely since they can be used with just about any subject.

SELECTING SOFTWARE

Issues to Consider

There is a lot of software to choose from and your computer lab won't need it all at once. Carefully consider these issues as you make your choices:

➢ Will the program attract and keep the learners' attention? It doesn't matter what the content is if the kids won't stick with the program long enough to learn it.

➢ Does the program teach something that's important for my students to learn? Our time in Christian education is limited and valuable. Consider how the program will coordinate with the rest of the curriculum.

➢ Is the program theologically and biblically appropriate?

➢ Does the program give the teacher and student choices in content selection? Look for programs that allow you to fast forward, skip, or jump to certain sections. This is important not only in terms of content selection but in managing class time.

➢ Does the program offer an opportunity for learner and teacher input, output, or the option to change content? Software with content preference controls, printable databases, and question editors add versatility.

➢ Does the program offer varying degrees of difficulty? Can you adjust the content to meet the needs of different age groups?

➢ Does the program "pull" the student through its material, encouraging them to move through content, or does the program merely let them wander about? For example, King David invites students to follow him as he tells his story in *Pathways through Jerusalem. A Walk in the Footsteps* has "secret passage-ways" that move students to the next area. Other programs have less "pull," but can be successfully used with worksheets that help "push" students toward specific areas of a program.

➤ Will my students want to use the program a second time, or a third time?

➤ Can more than one student enjoy this program at the same time? This is a very important issue given the expense of hardware and need to keep your hardware-to-student ratios in correct proportion (1 to 3).

➤ Will the program fit in the class time I have available?

➤ Will the program run well on the equipment I have? A great program can be a disaster on a slow computer.

How Much Software Will I Need?

The amount of software you need to purchase depends on the number of computers you have, the kind of computers you have, the age range of students using the lab, and how often students will be using the lab.

If you are working with elementary age students, start with two or three titles, build to five or six titles for the year, and add perhaps two or three new titles each year. These numbers begin to increase as your computer lab is used by learners in other age groups. Some churches use a lot of software. All work to make the most of the amount they can afford. The nice thing about most good software is that you can use it year after year.

It is best to purchase one copy of each program for each computer in your lab. This may seem like a luxury, but I encourage you to indulge! Two or three computers in a lab each running a different software program is a recipe for chaos and teacher frustration. It also makes lesson planning for the entire class a challenge. The only way around purchasing one copy of each program for each computer is to have a separate teacher for each piece of software in use. In the long run, you'll find it easier to teach when everyone is working on the same program. There is an exception to this rule. In some cases students can rotate among different computers that are running different programs touching on the same subject. Purchasing extra software is also easier than finding extra teachers.

There are two approaches to collecting software. One is what I call the "library" approach. Churches using this approach enjoy collecting software from which they make up their lesson plans. They may purchase an interesting program just to see what they might be able to do with it in connection with their curriculum. Other churches take a more selective approach. They select software as needed based on the objectives and scope and sequence of their curriculum. There is merit to each approach. The selective approach assumes familiarity with software and usually a small software budget. The "library" approach can produce some unexpected surprises as teachers explore new possibilities.

I encourage churches to be selective at first, but to stay flexible enough to explore interesting pieces of software with their learners without always needing to know the outcome.

> *The amount of software you need to purchase depends on the number of computers you have, the kind of computers you have, the age range of students using the lab, and how often students will be using the lab.*

Theological Issues

Understandably, we all want to know the theological perspective of software before we buy it or use it. This review can be difficult with software since demos or review copies are not readily available. Even knowledge about the publisher's theological position doesn't always help. Those publishing or distributing the program aren't necessarily the ones creating the content. Even a program that I have reviewed and approved occasionally may say something a little differently than I'd prefer. I personally view this as an opportunity for class discussion.

The place software tends to be easiest to assess for its theology is in the Bible research tools. In these Bible programs, the developers employ—and document for you, the user—a wide variety of reference books, study helps, and other research tools. Review the lists of source material used in developing the software to find Bible research tools that meet your needs. These Bible tools are widely publicized by denominations and independent catalogs and magazines. Many of them, however, may not be age-appropriate for children or youth.

Selecting Quiz-Making Software

One of the important contributions computers are making to Christian education is their ability to encourage lesson recall in a kid-friendly manner. Teachers often move from one lesson to the next without much time given to refreshing their learners' memories. By making use of computer quiz programs like *Journey, Grand Slam,* and *Sunday School Tutor,* you can test, reinforce, and promote recall of lessons on a regular basis. The kids find it enjoyable, are proud of what they can remember, and it tells you which subjects are mastered, misunderstood, or need to be taught again. Your learners will enjoy coming up with their own quizzes based on lessons for themselves or their classmates.

Quizzes are a great way to enhance the content of more game-oriented software. With a quiz or computer tutorial, you can pull out certain information from a game and expand on its content. This can happen before or after the game software is used. When I tell my kids that they have to get 80 percent or better on the quiz before they can continue the game, they don't mind at all. It's the computer!

Creatively written tutorials and reviews can introduce new information and test for it in the same sitting. "Computer-based training" multimedia tutorials are a growing part of the public school and business world's use of computers. It is an educational tool with benefits for Christian education programs as well. See Chapter 6 for more information on creating and using quizzes.

How Hardware Affects Software Selection

As previously mentioned, older hardware limits software choices. Plan on moving to equipment that is CD-capable as soon as possible. Starting with older CD-capable machines will allow you to run today's software recommendations, but maybe not tomorrow's.

Ideally, have all your hardware running at the same level of capability. Placing older and newer hardware side by side in the computer lab usually proves frustrating to the kids and teachers. It is hard to get kids to concentrate at a computer that's not CD-capable when the multimedia monster is roaring next to them. Having matched hardware is an issue of flexibility versus limits.

Other Selection Factors

When making a purchase, be aware that "first looks" can be deceiving, especially if you are not yet an experienced software teacher. Some programs, which at first don't look so great, work well with the right approach and lesson plan. *Wordy* is one such example. At first look, I thought the kids would throw it back at me. As it turned out, they loved adding their own material and then playing the memory game with it.

On several occasions, I've previewed or used a program without much hope, only to discover new approaches to it or to receive good advice from another teacher. On the other hand, some programs have all the bells and whistles but don't work well in the classroom for one reason or another. Parson's *Jonah and the Whale* CD is an example of this kind. It's a nice program, but the format doesn't work well for most Christian education programs. (It takes over an hour for early readers to complete, there's no way to skip any of its activities, and you can't bookmark your spot and pick it up in another session.)

Occasionally, you may need to use a piece of software that seems rather dull on its own but serves a necessary purpose in your lesson plan. *Quickverse* and *Compton's Bible* are two such examples. The kids won't get too excited about searching *Quickverse* for examples of thanksgiving in the Psalms. But it can be important preparation for having them write and illustrate their own thanksgiving psalm in *Kidworks*.

Certain programs are good selections for a later stage in your computer lab development rather than early on.

Finally, be conscious of your own preferences in software selection. For example, don't automatically exclude game programs from your lab just because you're not a "gamer." Most kids are gamers and they can learn through games. Games can also be used as incentives.

MULTIPLE COPIES, NETWORKING, AND SITE LICENSES

Almost every piece of Christian software has a clear copyright statement that limits you to using one purchased copy of the program on one computer at a time. Assume that all do, even if you cannot see the printed statement. This copyright precludes you from buying one copy of a program and making multiple copies of it for several computers or from attempting to use a network to link one program with several terminals. If you have three computers and want all the kids to be working on the same program at the same time, you will need to purchase three copies of the program.

In addition, the Christian software industry offers almost no "site licenses." Because the Christian software market is aimed mostly at the home market, and because programs are very reasonably priced, they are not inclined to offer site licenses and rarely offer quantity discounts for anything less than five to 10

> *Almost every piece of Christian software has a clear copyright statement that limits you to using one purchased copy of the program on one computer at a time.*

copies. Please share this information with your "techies"—those persons skilled in using hardware and software who will be your best friends in setting up a computer lab in your church. They may be surprised to hear this because of the prevalence of site licenses and network copies in the business world.

If you copy Christian software, you are almost always in violation of the commandment "You shall not steal," and the law. Someone will undoubtedly suggest to you that it is a common practice to illegally copy software and thus it is OK. If this happens, look the speaker squarely in the eye and remind him or her that we have a commandment about that. It is inappropriate to teach the gospel with stolen materials!

LAST WORDS ON SOFTWARE

➢ There is no substitute for previewing the software with kids present to test their initial reactions.

➢ Take time to create terrific lesson plans that incorporate the software.

➢ Look for software that works with the rest of your curriculum.

➢ Ask your denominational or ecumenical resource center to preview software or keep a list of programs recommended by others in your area.

➢ Network with others purchasing and using software to share ideas.

➢ Buy software on the recommendation of what you can see or someone you trust. If this isn't possible and you must buy sight unseen, insist on a return policy.

➢ Preview other people's software at their site.

➢ Request software reviews in the Christian education publications you read. Ask that reviews be completed by people who are actually teaching with computers.

➢ Send a list of software titles you like to your denominational education office or publisher so they can refer others to them.

➢ Help sponsor seminars on teaching with software.

➢ Send software back if you don't like it. Send it back even if the company won't refund your money. Let them know you care about quality.

➢ Write letters about software to the editor of your favorite Christian computing magazine.

➢ Write letters to the software producer and the distributor telling them exactly what you like, don't like, and want to see in the future.

➢ Teaching with computers isn't rocket science. This is about kids, content, and working with the right teachers. Let your teaching instincts and classroom experience guide you. Select your software carefully to match the circumstances of your start-up.

➢ Explore a variety of programs and approaches. Learn from your classroom successes and mistakes. This is a new medium. Don't expect to get it all right the first time. In my experience, churches need a full six months to a year to get comfortable with their computer labs.

Chapter 4

Questions and Answers about Hardware

Grab a cup of coffee, we're going to start talking hardware. If you are "technologically challenged," this chapter may look like alphabet and number soup. (If this is the case, read Chapter 10, "Computer 101 for the Technologically Challenged.") For all leaders who are planning a computer lab for Christian education, it will make life easier in the long run if you establish a close and friendly relationship with a computer techie (or techies) before you start. This person (or persons) will be invaluable in helping you to make hardware decisions, manage your equipment, and troubleshoot the problems. Make sure you befriend a real computer buff and not an "armchair techie." Armchair techies can talk a great game, but don't always know how to manage a system well or correct problems when they occur. Realize too, that before your techies can really help you, they need to understand the goals you have for the computer lab, how you plan for kids to use the lab, and the technical requirements of the software you are planning to use.

If you are a computer techie as well as as an education leader, you may find some of this chapter obvious. Read it anyway. It contains a number of important insights from techies in Christian education computer labs around the country. You'll also probably discover that the computing done in Christian education computer labs is different from the secular education and business world applications you may already know. In those worlds, each computer is usually being used by one person for periods of time longer than 55 minutes. Also, adults are more patient than kids with slow machines. And in the public schools, the teacher has greater leverage over student performance.

THE LONG VIEW OF HARDWARE

The computer hardware market is truly amazing. Prices are going down and selection is going up. Predicting the future can be difficult but fun. This chapter was written in the fall of 1997. Right now you can buy a brand new 180 MHz Pentium PC with 16 megabytes of RAM, a 12-speed CD-ROM drive, and a monitor for about $1,000. If you're looking to buy brand new, this would be the perfect machine for the budget conscious. It would also be able to run every piece of software mentioned in this book and then some. Why? The Christian software industry is not pushing the outer limits of hardware power (which is today around the 233 MHz level with a recommended 32 megabytes of RAM). Judging from discussions with a number of Christian software developers, the

Your Friend, the "Techie"

> *It will make life easier in the long run if you establish a close and friendly relationship with a computer techie (or techies) before you start.*

Pentium 180 will last you three to five years with only some inexpensive upgrades about every two years.

At the date of this book's publication, it is not recommended that you start your computer lab with older Macintosh computers unless that is what you already have available to you. Personal computers (also known as "IBM-compatible") are usually less expensive to purchase and more Christian software is available for them. This is especially true if you are starting with older, donated machines without CD drives. There was very little Christian software produced for older Macintosh models. Macintosh lovers, however, take heart! The gap is slowly closing. Almost all new software is both Windows and Macintosh compatible.

FREQUENTLY-ASKED QUESTIONS

Here are some of the most frequently asked questions about computer hardware for use in Christian education:

Question: **Aren't we talking about a lot of money here?**
Answer: Here's a list of potential donation and low-cost hardware sources for you to consider in the start-up stage of your computer lab.

➢ Computers donated by church members. There are more of them hanging around in closets than you can imagine. (For more information, read the section about upgrading older computers on page 28.)

➢ Local businesses and your members' employers. Businesses regularly upgrade their equipment and sometimes have like-new computers to give away.

➢ Refurbished, older model computers at modest prices. Check your local retailers.

➢ Church office or staff computers. Paying careful mind to turf wars and the legitimate fear of kids rifling church membership files, help folks remember that the kids' parents did pay for them and they usually aren't being used on Sundays or evenings. See if you can work out a deal.

➢ Laptop computers. Find someone who can bring theirs in for a couple of Sundays and hook it up to a larger external monitor. This is not a long-term solution, as you will read later, but can work for your experiment phase.

➢ New computers. Prices are surprisingly low and I never met a church that couldn't use one if, for some unimaginable reason, you decide not to set up a computer lab after the experiment stage.

➢ How about that secret benefactor? Some folks are waiting for just such an innovative project as a computer education lab.

➢ Memorial funds, church library funds.

➢ Check with your local computer shop. Some have been known to lend computers of one sort or another to churches in the hope of future business.

Be prepared! Educators and pastors everywhere are surprised by the kind of equipment they're finding in their congregations and communities. And be prepared for that someone in your congregation who will step up within the first year of your lab and offer their financial support. Often, this person is a computer techie thrilled to see you using a tool they enjoy. It might also be an older member of the congregation excited about the potential of happy kids and a commitment to Bible literacy.

In my church, our lab was started years ago with two new computers donated by a family whose grandmother had passed away. She had been a teacher and they wanted to make a memorial gift to something special and innovative in her name. When the success and excitement of using computers became apparent, the money for expansion started to flow from the education committee, church leaders, and supportive individuals. This story of support is being repeated all over the country.

Keep your sights high. When all is said and done, strive to start with equipment that meets or exceeds the current needs of the software you choose. Sometimes "making do" with less can bring frustration from kids and teachers, which can lead to diminished use or even abandonment of the project, thus confirming the naysayers' "See, this was a dumb idea after all."

Strive to start with equipment that meets or exceeds the current needs of the software you choose.

Question: *But I don't know anything about computers!*

Answer: There are probably more people in your congregation who are computer literate than Bible literate! As an education leader, you need to understand kids, teaching and learning processes, and the goals of your program. You don't need to understand technology as well. The computer lab will need a management and a teaching team, so start recruiting people to complement your strengths and cover for your weaknesses. Don't let the word *recruiting* scare you either. Many of your members have computer skills and will be eager to help. Computer people (techies) love to hang around computers.

Question: *How many computers will I need?*

Answer: Only one or two to start your experiment. After that, the number of computers you need will depend on your vision, goals, finances, and the number of students you plan to have using computers at one time.

In general, plan for one computer for every three students in your lab. With many software programs, two students per computer is the limit or you'll have anxious, frustrated kids who don't get their turn. There may be times when you would have just one student per computer, but in general I prefer the results of the cooperative learning that occurs with two or three learners working together with a software program. A few programs can accommodate teams of up to five students if the monitor is large enough.

There are two important factors that limit the number of kids you will want to put at each computer. First is the optimum viewing distance between a student and the monitor. If learners are more than three feet away, forget it. Second is the benefit of the interactive nature of computing. If a learner becomes only a spectator—instead of an active participant in working through the software—you might as well invest in a VCR. They are cheaper. Read more about these ratios in Chapters 5 and 6.

Question: *What kind of computers will I need?*

Answer: That depends on your budget and the kinds of programs you want to run. At this point, I recommend that you begin with CD-capable multimedia personal computers ("IBM-compatible"). Having PCs equipped with Windows 95 or its successor will allow you to choose from the entire marketplace of software. This will help your start-up experiment experience the real possibilities, rather than only guess at them.

As mentioned previously in this chapter, the Christian software industry has historically been PC. Newer CD software, however, is coming out in what is called a "hybrid" version, meaning it runs on both Macintosh and PC. Unless you've exhausted all other possibilities, I do not recommend starting with anything less than CD-capable computers.

Question: *What about using Macintosh computers?*

Answer: Macintoshes are great computers, but there are important issues to consider before making them the computer of choice for your lab. The first issue is price. New PCs are generally cheaper than new Macintoshes. And if you choose to run some of the older DOS and Windows software for Christian education on your Macintosh, you will need special software or hardware upgrades. This will add even more to the difference in price between a suitable PC and a suitable Macintosh.

If you already have CD-capable Macintoshes available in your church or you're a Macintosh-only kind of person, then by all means go with Macintosh for your lab. Just be prepared to spend some extra cash and to not be able to run easily some of the fine older programs that are still out there. Make sure your Macintosh has at least 16 megabytes of RAM to run multimedia.

If you do choose Macintosh as your computer system, please be aware that even though many early Macintoshes were CD-capable, they may not be able to run today's video- and graphic-intensive CDs. The following Macintosh computers should be able to run today's multimedia software just fine or with minimal upgrades: any 68040 or better, Power Macintosh series, or Quadra Macintosh series. The Performa series, LC II, and 68030 may be able to run CDs if so equipped and if they have at least 16 megabytes of RAM. Avoid the following Macintoshes for your computer lab: Macintosh II, Classic, Plus, LC series. In addition to their underperformance, there is very little, if any, Christian software available for them.

Question: *Can I use older PC computers?*

Answer: Possibly, but using older PCs will limit your software choices. There were some very nice DOS and Windows titles produced in years past that still are available today. They come on 3.5" diskettes and run on the relatively modest computers sold between 1991and 1994. By "modest" I mean a 386 or 486 with a power supply of 16, 20, 25, or 33 MHz, 4 or 8 megabytes of RAM, a hard drive in the 100-300 megabyte range, an 8-bit Soundblaster-compatible sound card, stereo speakers, a joystick, and a VGA monitor. If you plan to use older PC equipment, make sure it meets at least these standards. You can often find computers for donation that started out as 386s or 486s, but have since been upgraded with new processing chips, more RAM, and maybe even a CD-ROM drive.

With the abundance of upgraded 386's and 486's in the donation market, don't even bother with 286's. (They would, however, make interesting wall decorations—no kidding.) This advice applies to 386's without upgrades as well.

Question: ***Can I upgrade older computers effectively?***
Answer:　Sometimes yes, sometimes no. It depends on the type of computer, and the number and cost of the upgrades. Be very careful about spending money on upgrading computers. The general rule of thumb is not to spend more than one-third of the cost of a new computer (today that is about about $300-$400) on upgrading an older computer. It makes no sense when a brand-new unit sells for under $1,000. And depending on where you start and what you put in it, the upgrades may not get you anywhere near the computing power you need for the next year or two. The phrase, "penny-wise and pound-foolish" is particularly applicable to upgrading existing hardware.

I have met some hardware techies who can work wonders with older equipment. Some work in the industry and have access to free or low-cost parts. Sometimes they are a godsend. Sometimes the computers they build are more trouble than they are worth.

Question: ***Can I add a CD-ROM drive to a 486 or an older Macintosh?***
Answer:　Maybe, but it's not a simple answer. Some computers can be effectively upgraded to run CD-ROM. Some upgrades will cost too much money. The problem is that you shouldn't add a CD drive without also upgrading the other components needed to run software on CD. These other components can include: RAM, sound card, processor chip, and video card or driver. Be careful that you are not putting hotrod wheels on a buckboard.

For example, to run the CD-ROM software recommended in this book, your processor speed should be at least 66 MHz, preferably higher (which means faster). You also need a minimum of 8 megabytes of RAM and preferably 16. The CD drive should be at least an 8-speed (16 and 24 speeds are common to date). You need to make sure the sound card is a 16-bit stereo card and not an old 8-bit card. The hard drives on some older computers are ridiculously small (40 and 85 megabytes). Your hard drive should be no less than 300 megabytes and preferably much bigger in order to store the software and graphics you need.

Some parts can be replaced, some cannot because they are soldered onto the main board of the computer. Replacing a 33 MHz chip with a 66 or higher can work but, realistically, you are only upgrading to a minimum level. Always consult the computer manufacturer first and have this work done by an expert.

In some cases, to run CD-ROM software you may need to upgrade an older computer's monitor. This can mean replacing the monitor, or the video driver

The general rule of thumb is not to spend more than one-third of the cost of a new computer on upgrading an older computer.

software, or the video card itself. Most current CD-ROM programs output 256 colors to the screen or higher to create their colorful presentations. Older computers, monitors, software, and video cards may not be able to handle this amount of information going to the screen.

The upgrade rule of thumb is $300-$400, or one-third the cost of a new computer. With some computers you'll be over that in a heartbeat. You may be better off taking that donated 486 and running only non-CD software on it until you can make the jump into true multimedia hardware.

Question: **Can I make at least some effective use of an old 386 or 486?**

Answer: To a certain degree. Some of my favorite software titles are the older ones. These older computers can be a great way to get started for little money. Make sure that the computer in question has Windows 3.1 on it and at least an 8-bit sound card. The only potential problem may come when you put a CD-capable computer next to the old one in the lab. Kids will be kids!

Some churches make use of their older equipment by using it only for certain software, like games and quiz programs. One church built a "Komputer Kwiz Kave" out of cardboard and twinkle lights and turned their old 386 into a testing station.

When you receive a donated, used computer, have a qualified technician or computer techie take a look at it. Make sure the hard drive is cleaned of old files and any potential viruses or glitches. In many cases, it is wise to pay a little money to have a professional do the work.

A "Komputer Kwiz Kave"

Question: **What if I'm buying a new computer?**

Answer: I'd buy a mid-range multimedia CD-capable computer. At the time of this book's writing, a mid-range computer is defined as a 150-180 MHz chip with 16 megabytes of RAM and an 8- or 12-speed CD-ROM drive. Consult with your resident techie to determine the current mid-range.

The Christian software developers are not producing anything for the top echelon of computing power. This trend will continue for the foreseeable future. Why? Their market is still small and that means they cannot afford to invest the kind of dollars needed to produce the kind of videos and graphics a powerful computer would be able to handle. They will, however, continue to move forward. Fortunately, today's new multimedia computers are designed to accommodate upgrades far more easily than the 386 and 486 PCs and older Macintoshes were.

Question: **Should I consider purchasing laptop computers?**

Answer: No. They are more expensive than desktops and their limited viewing area is a drawback to multiple users. They are also more expensive to repair and upgrade, and they're more susceptible to damage. They can, however, be a great way to get started in your experiment stage if someone is willing to bring theirs in for a couple of Sundays.

Question: **Why is a bigger and faster computer generally better?**

Answer: Today's CD-ROM programs require a lot of memory and speed to deliver effectively their wonderful graphics, video, sound, and text. If your computer doesn't have enough memory or speed, the program will run with delays in the picture and sound. The technology is changing rapidly to enable software content to become richer, deeper, and more interactive.

Question: **Will I need a printer?**

Answer: Yes, eventually you will want one or more. Color printers are relatively inexpensive these days and sometimes come bundled with new computer purchases. Many programs allow the teachers and students to print out materials in color or black and white. For example, with *Kidworks Deluxe* your students can print out their Bible storybooks to take home. Black inkjet printers are in the donation market as are older dot matrix printers. You might even find some color inkjets for donation, but be aware that color inkjet cartridges are a bit more expensive than black. Don't bother with dot matrix printers.

Networking multiple computers to a single printer is a popular choice in church computer labs. This can be done rather easily with a mechanical two- or three-way switch box. It can also be done using more sophisticated wires and electronic switches.

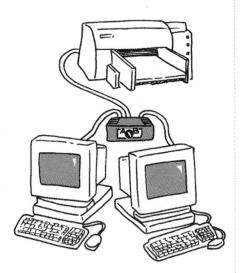

Two Computers Linked by Wire to an A/B Switch Box

Question: **What about networking our computers to a main unit?**

Answer: Most of the software copyrights preclude you from doing this unless you have purchased a copy of the program you are networking for each computer station on the network. While it is rather common in the business world, colleges, and schools to wire all the computers to a central network server where users access one licensed network copy of a program, the Christian software industry at this point has written its copyrights for single computer use. The relatively low price of the software makes it unattractive for them to even consider offering site licenses.

Networking can be expensive. In general, I do not recommend it unless you have more than six computers and plenty of congregational expertise (a whole team of techies).

Networking can, however, be a reasonable solution for hardware and operating system management if you have more than six computers. In this case, having all your computers wired together allows your hardware management team to make changes in items such as menus and drivers all at once. You would still need to buy individual pieces of software for each computer. Make sure you have a whole team of techies who know what they're doing if you take this route. Do not make your entire system dependent on the good graces and expertise of one individual.

Question: ***Will I need Windows 3.1, Windows 95, or the latest Windows version?***
Answer: If you are running 486 and 386 computers with 8 megabytes of RAM or less and with no CD drive, then Windows 3.1 will suffice. To run most CD software, you're better off with Windows 95 or its successor. In many cases, it will be installed already on your donated or new computer. Windows 95 and its successor will run both DOS and Windows programs, but it is recommended that you run it only on a faster 486 or higher processor with a minimum 16 megabytes of RAM. Newer PCs will come with Windows 95 or its successor. These newer versions of Windows take the headaches out of hardware management by automatically handling most installation and configuration issues for you behind the scenes.

Question: ***What about buying a modem and hooking up to the Internet?***
Answer: This is a great idea down the line in your computer journey. Connecting, communicating, and researching via the Internet is the next frontier for the computers in Christian education. Many churches have already begun their explorations. Read Chapter 8 for more Internet information.

Question: ***What kind of monitors will we need?***
Answer: The current standard is the 15" monitor. However, many churches are stretching to purchase 17" monitors to increase the viewing area for multiple student use. Be aware that older computers typically come with 14" and 13" monitors. Their picture resolution is usually lower in quality too, due to limitations in their technology. The monitor is the "business end" of the computer, and yet it's the one equipment purchase where people tend to cut corners. Don't. Monitor prices are dropping, like everything else related to computers. Shop around.

Question: ***Any recommendations on how to buy a computer?***
Answer: Yes. Buy a computer at a local business that has technical support at that location. Be cautious when buying discount computers via the mail. If you run into problems, you could be in for a long wait for service. Regarding brand names, buy those with good reputations. Ask your well-read techies to give you some thoughts on which brands to buy.

HARDWARE AND SOFTWARE BUDGETING

Every computer lab needs a budget. Here are a few general guidelines.

Software

Individual programs will cost between $10 and $60, with the average being around $30 per program. If you're dreaming of a nicely-stocked computer lab, plan on spending $150 to $200 per workstation on software to get started and perhaps another $100 per station each year for three new programs. If you are following the optimum setup recommendation by purchasing multiple copies of each software for each of your computers, budget accordingly. These budget figures do not include operating system expenses (such as upgrading to the new version of Windows).

Hardware

It is recommended that you budget about $150 a year per computer for routine hardware maintenance and repairs. Mice break, but are inexpensive to replace. Sometimes hard drives break. This can easily blow your entire annual budget. Monitors can cost between $200 and $500 to replace. The older the equipment you begin with, the higher the maintenance and replacement budget you should have.

Budget for upgrades, whether you are using new or used computers. Use the budgeted funds for more RAM memory chips, faster CD drives, or a sound card. Prices continue to drop for these kinds of equipment upgrades. Expect to pay about $200-$500 per machine every two to three years for needed upgrades.

Also, think down the road to when you'll replace your computers. If you're beginning with older equipment, this road is short. If you're beginning with new equipment, you should plan to seriously upgrade them in two to three years and replace them in about four to six years. This recommendation may change with technological innovations. Fortunately, innovation rarely makes good software unusable.

Other Hardware Issues

Mouse or Trackball?

Each computer will need a mouse. However, you may want to consider trackballs instead of mice. A trackball looks like a mouse except that it has a large marble on top that is rolled by the fingers to control the screen cursor. Mice must roll around on a hard surface. This means the person seated by the mouse usually ends up being in control of the program unless students agree to play musical chairs. A trackball can easily be passed around and held in a student's hand or lap. If you plan on having more than two students at a computer, consider trackballs. They will help foster sharing and cooperative behavior. Also, trackballs are easier for younger kids to use.

Speakers

You will need speakers. Buy ones that sound good at low volume. Be sure they have the volume knob right on the speaker case, instead of volume control through an onscreen control. If speakers don't sound good at low volume, kids usually crank them up. Your computer lab teachers—and those in adjoining classrooms—will thank you for good, low-volume speakers and a little sound-proofing in the classroom.

Budget for upgrades, whether you are using new or used computers.

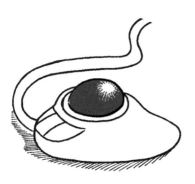

A trackball doesn't require a hard surface and can easily be passed around to facilitate sharing of computer control.

Joysticks

You may want to purchase game pads or joysticks for each computer for use with certain games, even though most games can be played with the keyboard instead of a game pad. A microphone will also come in handy for recording sound effects in programs such as Kidworks. Some computers come with a built-in microphone.

System Backup

It is strongly recommended that you buy a backup tape drive to prevent loss of important data from your hard drive in the event of a computer crash. There are many different kinds of backup systems and each year seems to bring new options.

Anti-Virus

You'll also need a current virus protection program. This will cost you around $50. Computer viruses can easily be brought in from outside diskettes and off the Internet, destroying your system and causing hours of extra work and headaches.

Routine Maintenance

Remember those techies you need to recruit to join your computer lab team? You'll need them to keep your hardware and operating system working efficiently. Programs and files get misplaced, develop glitches, or need to be reloaded. Unless you actually enjoy defragging (defragmenting) your hard drive, computer techies come in handy. (As hard drives work, they tend to scatter files around the disk. *Defragging* is a bit of reorganizing and housecleaning that every computer needs from time to time in order to regain efficiency.)

Routine maintenance can extend the life of your computer. Have your techie remove the cover of your older computer and carefully clean the dust bunnies off the motherboard. This will help reduce heat buildup around old parts. Keep Sunday school glitter, glue, and magnets, as far away from your computers as possible. Use high-quality surge protectors with your electrical outlets to protect against power surges in the electrical lines and lightning strikes.

Think through your hardware decisions carefully. Start where you can. Make a plan that gets you where you want to be.

HARDWARE SUMMARY

The right hardware and a workable budget can make or break your successful use of computers in Christian education, especially in your start-up phase. Having a plan to add to or upgrade your equipment is essential to your vision. Creating a schedule for equipment upgrades and replacement may be a new concept for your church. The capabilities of your computer hardware will directly affect the message you can present. Think through your hardware decisions carefully. Start where you can. Make a plan that gets you where you want to be.

Summary of Upgrade and Purchasing Issues

286 — Not recommended for use or upgrading.

386/16, 20 MHz — Typically has 1 to 8 RAM capacity. Can be upgraded to include an 8-bit sound card, Windows 3.1, and additional RAM to run older software programs. Recommended for your computer lab only if all other possibilities are exhausted.

486/20, 25, 33 MHz — Typically comes with 8 megabytes of RAM or less. Usually comes with Windows 3.1 operating system. This level of computer often received upgrades by the original user. Some, but not all, can be upgraded with a new processing chip, RAM, and CD drive to run CD programs published prior to 1997.

486/50, 66 or Pentium 75 and 90 MHz chips — Will have at least 8 megabytes of RAM. Usually has either Windows 3.1 or Windows 95. Can usually be upgraded with a CD-ROM drive if it doesn't already have one. If upgraded, can run most CDs published in 1995 to 1997 quite nicely. May have some performance problems (slow transitions, for example) with video on most current CDs.

100, 133, 150, 166, 166 MMX, 180 MHz processor speeds and higher — Usually have at least 16 megabytes of RAM with at least 8-speed CD drives and Windows 95 or higher. Commonly referred to as "multimedia-capable computers." Will run every Christian software CD on the market to date very well.

Summary of Macintosh hardware recommendations — These Macintosh computers will handle all of the Christian software CDs: Power Mac series, 68040 chip series, Quadra series. At most they may need some extra RAM or faster CD drive.

These Macintosh computers will handle some of the Christian software CDs, although to run them well, they will probably need some upgrades: the 68030 series Macintoshes, the LC II and Performa series. Video replay performance in the 68030 series may be slow depending on a number of factors.

These Macintoshes are not recommended for use: Macintosh II, IIe, Classic, Plus, LCs.

Creating a Bible Computer Lab

This chapter presents a number of important issues related to setting up and using computers in your Christian education program. The remarks are aimed primarily at computer labs for Sunday school use. However, those of you exploring other uses for computers in your program, such as confirmation, weekday fellowship meetings, or a tutoring center for neighborhood children will find the advice just as helpful.

WHAT IS A BIBLE COMPUTER LAB?

A Bible computer lab is a special place in the church where students and specially trained teachers use computers as the main delivery medium or as a component of a Christian education session. It is a place where computer hardware and software are concentrated, rather than having equipment diffused throughout the church facility. It is a place where different groups of children and youth are scheduled to come in for computer-assisted instruction related to their ongoing curriculum or for enrichment activities in addition to the regular curriculum. It is a place that can become the most popular hangout in the church. It is a place that attracts attention and showcases your commitment to the evangelism and nurture of a new generation.

A Bible computer lab can consist of one computer, three, five, ten, or more. It can involve elementary-age children, youth, or adult classes. It can be the corner of your educator's office. It even can be in the church office while you are getting started. The key concept is that it is a place where the students are taught by specially assigned teachers trained in this medium. As your vision and amount of equipment grows, find a secure, permanent place for your lab.

The lab's computers can be used for Sunday morning classes, weekday or evening programs, fellowship groups, Bible study groups, confirmation, summer vacation Bible school, or for independent study.

Some churches also use their labs for mission and outreach, such as tutoring programs for neighborhood children or a computer training center to assist individuals seeking to upgrade their job skills. Some churches incorporate their computers into the church library, making them available to the members of the congregation for individual study and reference.

In the church where I first began teaching with computers, we had a separate room called the Bible Computer Lab. Our five computers were used on a rotating basis by Grades 1-6 throughout our Sunday morning schedule all year

> *A Bible computer lab is a special place in the church where students and trained lab teachers come together to learn, using Christian software and related lesson materials.*

long. Our teens served as teaching assistants, though they occasionally had their own lab class time. We used our computers in three different Sunday morning time slots for children before, after, and during Sunday school. This wide variety of use and student groupings led us to value having plenty of hardware, copies of software for each computer, and plenty of extra help.

Taming the 800-Pound Gorilla

While it is currently popular in public education to put "computers in every classroom," this approach doesn't seem to work for most churches. Neither does putting one computer in the corner of one classroom. The problem is that the computer is the proverbial 800-pound gorilla in the room. If the computer is running in the corner of a classroom, that's where all your kids will want to be.

There is another reason why most churches have created Bible computer labs and moved away from putting computers in classrooms. Volunteer teachers who already feel rushed to prepare their regular lesson often view use of the computer as a break from teaching or a reward for good behavior. And because they are not specifically trained in teaching with the software, many learning opportunities are missed or frittered away by not using the software to its fullest. For most churches, concentrating lessons with computers and software in the Bible computer lab has proven to be the best way to make the most of these tools.

DIFFERENT LAB CONCEPTS

There are two main ways to approach teaching with computers in your computer lab: everyone working together on the same subject (the classroom model) or everyone working independently (the independent study zone model). They are not mutually exclusive and each comes with its own plusses, minuses, and variations. Over time you will, no doubt, incorporate many elements of both as you gain experience and further explore how computers can be used in your program. A third lab concept is that of "game room."

Everyone Working Together

Most churches primarily use their lab as a special Sunday morning classroom. A different group of kids rotates into the lab each week (or for two weeks in a row). After group study and discussion, they fan out to their computer stations and all work on the same program at the same time, as teachers and assistants work with them. After a certain period of time, the class reassembles for discussion and other related activities. Teachers find this design easiest to get started with and easiest to manage because all the kids are working on the same subject at the same time. This is in contrast to having different pieces of software running on each computer at the same time, although there may be times when learners can rotate among different programs during class time. Rotating different classes into the lab helps keep the need for software variety at a more reasonable level, since the same students are not in the lab all the time.

There are two main ways to approach teaching with computers in your computer lab: everyone working together on the same subject (the classroom model) or everyone working independently (the independent study zone model).

The Lab as an Independent Study Zone

A number of churches have designed their computer labs for independent study. Learners are assigned individually to certain weeks in the lab to complete a list of assigned programs. The plan is laid out in agreement between teacher and learner. Progress on the plan is tracked and charted in the computer lab. Pairs of students may be teamed at the station with a teacher or assistant who has a special knowledge of the program and facilitates its use and discussion. In the independent model, more student motivation is needed, as well as caring adult guidance in the software use. Left alone, kids will be kids.

This model is more labor-intensive than the classroom model. It requires more volunteers and training, more scheduling, and individual student management. This model still requires the teacher to be a guide. It does, however, solve many issues concerning too many kids, too few computers, or the lack of multiple copies of the same software for each station. Most churches who use this model use it in conjunction with the classroom "everyone working together" model.

The Lab as Game Room

There is a third lab concept called the "lab as game room." While there are times when your lab will certainly function like this, it seems an awful waste of money and opportunity to assemble computers just so kids can play games to pass some time. Still, there are times when your lab can be used to entertain kids while parents are in meetings or drinking that second cup of coffee. Make sure such time is supervised, and have kids use Christian game software instead of your educational lesson software in order to avoid overexposure to programs they may use when in the lab during regularly scheduled Sunday school times.

Where to Start

Most churches have had greater initial success with the lab as classroom model with everyone working on the same program at the same time. They have found it easier to get additional hardware and software than to constantly recruit, manage, and plan for independent study.

While your situation may ultimately be different, it is recommended that you begin with a small version of the lab classroom model and implement elements of the independent study zone model as time and resources permit. Lesson planning and room setup issues will be discussed later in this chapter.

WAYS TO USE YOUR BIBLE COMPUTER LAB

Whether you set up your computer lab as a classroom or as an independent study zone, there are several ways to incorporate use of the lab into your Christian education program. These include: Sunday morning classroom, extended session and weekday programming, confirmation, adult study, and tutoring.

Sunday Morning Classroom

By far, the most popular way to use computers is as a special classroom on Sunday morning. Most churches create a rotation schedule bringing different Sunday school classes into the lab over a period of time.

Some churches focus all their computing efforts on certain grades, usually upper elementary or junior high. Lesson plans are designed to coordinate the software with the topics of study in the regular curriculum. Read Chapter 6 for more information.

Extended Session and Weekday Programming

Some churches use their computer labs as activity stations for Sunday "extended session," that time after children have been in Sunday school and worship. Those serving children in weekday fellowship groups may use it in a similar way.

The "extended session" is how I first began using computers. We needed something that didn't feel like a class but was still educational. We often had the same group of kids and the class was composed of several different ages. This time slot can be a great way to get your lab rolling. The educational pressure is off and you can do some experimenting with different approaches.

Computers and Confirmation

New software is continually coming to the market, and while there are no specific programs for confirmands yet, there are some that can be adapted. *Giants of the Faith,* for example, introduces students to many of the Reformation's main heroes. This program could be used by a pastor and several students to open up discussion of this time in history. Some of the Bible reference software could be used like this as well.

Would you like to have all your confirmands know the Apostles' Creed, Lord's Prayer, or books of the Bible? Quiz-making tools, such as *Sunday School Tutor* and *Wordy,* help add some fun and motivation to this kind of memorization work. In fact, with a little bit of training, youth can make their own tutorials for themselves, each other, or for younger students.

You may have several people in your congregation well-versed in the use of multimedia presentation programs such as *Powerpoint* (Microsoft). Your learners may have already been exposed to this program and others like it (such as Apple's *Hyperstudio)* in school. If this is the case, you're closer than you might think to having your students create wonderful presentations about their faith, the Bible, and their views on the church.

The typical confirmand has to complete several service and study projects during his or her course of study. Assisting in the computer lab is a great service opportunity. Youth are some of the most computer literate people in our society. This could also be a training program for future lab teachers.

> *The most popular way to use computers is as a special classroom on Sunday morning.*

Adult Study

Look out kids, here come the grown-ups! One look at a program like *Pathways through Jerusalem* or some Bible study software, and adults will want a piece of the action, too. Adults of all ages and in all types of study groups are starting to ask for computer lab time in many churches. Teachers also may request access to the computer lab to help their lesson planning during the week. By the way, these folks are also a great source of lab teachers!

Tutoring

Depending on the needs of your community, you may find ways for your computer lab to offer an important service to those in need of access to a computer for upgrading job skills or for after-school homework and tutoring. Quite a few churches are doing just this and have found that the mission emphasis encourages more generous donations of funds for hardware and software.

There are many excellent tutoring resources available for most of the software that is frequently used in business and education. Check with local schools, businesses, and the employment office to determine which software tutoring would be of most value in your area. Find lab teachers who have experience tutoring as well as experience with the specific software being used. Contact another church or organization in your area that is already offering such a service and ask for help in setting up your tutoring lab. Find ways to offer flexible hours that will meet the needs of the learners.

Other Computer Lab Uses

Depending on your schedule of church activities, there may be other programs that would benefit from educational time in the computer lab. Many churches open their labs on Sunday night after a worship service or fellowship gathering. Others make lab time available for the children of those attending committee meetings or choir practice.

Initially, however, I recommend that churches reserve the energy for planning and coordination of their computer labs exclusively for the program identified as having the greatest need. This usually means Sunday school. Making the computers a special attraction on Sunday morning can help boost attendance not only in classes, but also in worship. Fellowship and weekday programs usually have more freedom to do activities that Sunday school can't do because of space, time, and clothing issues.

Sharing Computer Labs with Other Programs

Those churches with preschool programs or day-care centers (for children or adults) will find a myriad of opportunities for shared usage of a computer lab. If you go this route, be sure that the leaders of all programs involved agree on the parameters of schedule, budget, maintenance, and computer lab supervision.

Sharing equipment can sometimes lead to additional funding sources, expanding the capabilities of the computer lab for all involved.

If you have a Christian school in your facility, there may be computer equipment available for use on the weekends and evenings. Some of their hardware and software may be suitable for getting you started. However, the hardware and software setup they have designed to meet their teaching objectives may not work for yours. It is certainly worth an exploratory conversation to see how the computer workstations might be shared, keeping in mind, of course, the need to agree on guidelines for scheduling, budgeting, maintenance, and supervision. In many cases, schools located in churches are funded separately from the programs of the congregation. Be aware of this as you negotiate shared usage and expenses.

RATIOS: COMPUTERS TO STUDENTS TO TEACHERS

This section contains one of the most important pieces of advice I give to churches who come to me seeking help with computers. It is the issue raised most frequently. Unlike the traditional classroom setting, where adding two or three more kids is usually not a big concern, in the computer lab it matters. Having the right mix of computers, software, teachers, and students is extremely important to the successful use of the computer lab, especially in the beginning. I have met with a lot of teachers in churches where this advice was not heeded. Most speak of being overwhelmed, under-prepared, and frustrated.

Before launching your lab, you need to do a reality check. How large is your team of techies and teachers? How deep is your level of financial support? How many computer lab teachers and assistants can you realistically train and have present for each lab session?

In general, you will need one computer for every two or three learners in your lab. You need at least one lead teacher in the lab. This person plans the lessons, introduces the activity to learners, and leads the follow-up discussion and activities. You'll need additional teachers if you have more than four computers.

Plan on one lab assistant for every one to two computers. (Your teacher can double as one of the assistants.) These persons are there, ready to help learners as they work at the computer stations. For example, if your lab has three computer workstations and you have two or three kids at each one, your lab needs one lead teacher and one assistant. If you have younger students in the lab, you may need a lab assistant for each workstation.

If you are using the independent study model to organize your lab, you will need more computers and more teachers. "Independent" doesn't mean "independent of a teacher."

It makes no sense to make an investment in hardware and software and then shortchange the most crucial aspect of your lab—your teaching team. Having too few teachers for the number of students turns your teachers into "fire fighters" who spend their time running between computers. Ideally, you want to

> It makes no sense to make an investment in hardware and software and then shortchange the most crucial aspect of your lab—your teaching team.

Suggested Computer/Teacher Ratios		
Number of Computers*	Number of Lead Teachers	Assistants
1	1	0
2	1	1
3	1	1
4	1	2
5	2	1
6	2	2

*Assumes 2-3 students per computer
Younger students may require more assistant help.

create a situation where your teachers can fulfill their role as "guide by the side," teaching as the software is used.

Happily, most churches are discovering computer lab teachers easy to come by. The typical church will find quite a few people interested in this new way of teaching, attracted by the technology, fascinated by the software, and ready for the challenge. If support from an adequate number of teachers isn't there, you need to regroup and look for other, less teacher-intensive ways, to nurture your vision.

The software you select may also affect your lab ratios, design, and setup. Some programs, such as *Bible Atlas*, work well with one or two students, but not with three. A program like *Pathways through Jerusalem* could have two to four kids viewing it if the monitor is big enough, provided they each share in the control of the material.

Even with quizzes, I rarely have students take them alone. The opportunity for discussion about possible answers is an important one. As a teacher, I am never far from those taking or making quizzes.

SETTING UP YOUR LAB

As you begin the essential planning for a lab, keep these general pointers in mind:

➤ Right from the start, have the right number of computers for the number of kids who will be coming into the lab. If you don't have enough equipment, get creative about reducing the number of kids in the lab.

➤ Begin thinking now where you can put your permanent computer lab. Computers need space and security.

Finding a Place for Your Lab

If you are starting with one or two computers and a handful of kids, your lab can fit in a small room or end of a room. Be prepared, however, to outgrow

Computers Don't Like Glitter!

that space. If you absolutely have no place to grow into, you may want to limit or come up with a creative alternate plan for using computers in your education program. A version of the independent study model would work better in a situation of limited space and computers rather than trying to squeeze an entire class of learners into a cramped space.

If you will be starting with 10 or more students and three or more computers—or anticipate you will be getting to that point soon—go ahead and find a designated computer lab room now. If your space is used by other groups at other times in the week, plan a way to secure and cover your computers.

If your lab will be in a day school or Sunday school classroom, ban glitter from it now! Glitter and computers don't mix.

Determining Adequate Lab Space

You not only need room for your computers, you also need room for discussion and other learning activities during your lab sessions. Ideally, plan for a discussion area away from the computers.

Cooperative learning requires space in front of the computers. So, don't arrange your computers too close together. Plan for four to five feet between workstations. Computers also put out a surprising amount of heat. Your lab room will need plenty of ventilation.

One way to improve a small, noisy room is to create sight and sound buffers around your computers. This will allow them to be closer to each other while keeping distractions down to a minimum. Some churches make use of cubicles

Homemade Cubicles

or short walls. A little plywood will go a long way quite inexpensively. Attach foam and staple colorful fabric to the boards. Stand them on the floor or fasten them to your tables so that they project out into the room a bit to create cubbyholes. Keep the height of the cubicle low enough so the lead teacher can see what everyone's doing. Kids enjoy the feeling of a special area. Cubicles can be a terrific addition to any lab, especially those using the independent study model. Stiff, heavy foam board covered with cloth also makes a fine inexpensive divider. These can be cut to sit on the floor, fit around the table, and connect to a wall clip for stability. When not needed, they can be stacked in the corner.

Because the computer lab is often a "Johnny-come-lately" to space assignments in your church, it can sometimes be relegated to leftover areas that are unsuitable. Disputes over prime space can also be a problem. Don't let these deter you, however. Work with all involved to create the optimum space for your computer lab. This can set the stage for optimum learning and remove some impediments to a fast start.

ARRANGING YOUR COMPUTERS IN THE LAB

Unlike some other forms of teaching and learning where room layout may not be a critical issue, computers require special attention.

Computers Need Room

Plan to use tables for your computer lab workstations. Shared computers need tables where kids can spread out their Bibles and worksheets. Tables also make all the kids feel like they are in front of the computer and part of the action. Don't plan to use computer furniture or computer carts. They tend to be created for single users and you want to make each student at the workstation feel involved.

If various age groups will be using your computers, you will need to consider carefully furniture sizes. Big kids don't like to sit in little chairs. Folding chairs will work fine. Computer chairs can be more trouble than they are worth, especially when your students discover wheeled chairs on tiled floors!

More importantly, experiment with different heights of tables and chairs to accomplish the most comfortable working combination for different sizes of learners. Make sure monitors are at a kid-friendly height. Keep in mind that for the best computing posture (one that is easiest on backs, eyes, neck, and wrists), the top of the monitor should be at—or slightly below—the eye level of the user.

Computers Create Sound

Spacing computer workstations four to five feet apart is a necessity. Find ways to place sound-absorbing materials around the computing area and carpet on the floor. Proper spacing will also encourage kids to focus on what they are doing instead of what everyone else is doing.

Arrangement Variations: Perimeter and Pod

There are two popular ways to arrange computers in the Bible computer lab. The most popular is to place computers on tables around the perimeter of the room with the screens facing toward the center of the room. This arrangement gives the teacher a line of sight to see all the monitors and all the learners in the lab from one location, usually the center of the room. It also focuses student attention on their own station and puts distance between each computer's speakers. Cubicles or dividers can be used around each workstation, but make them no higher than about four feet.

A computer pod in the center of the room is another configuration used by some churches. In the pod arrangement, the backs of the computers face each other and the screens point toward the walls. Most often, low cubicle walls separate computers and students from each other. The main advantage of this arrangement is reduction of noise and student distraction of one another. The main disadvantage is for the teacher who cannot see what everyone is doing. The pod arrangement is popular among those using the independent study model and those with plenty of lab assistants.

The Office Lab

If your computer is in a church office, bring along a sheet to cover up the desk or other off-limit areas to keep little fingers from wandering. Have the class decorate the sheet with a computer motif. They could even list what they are learning on it.

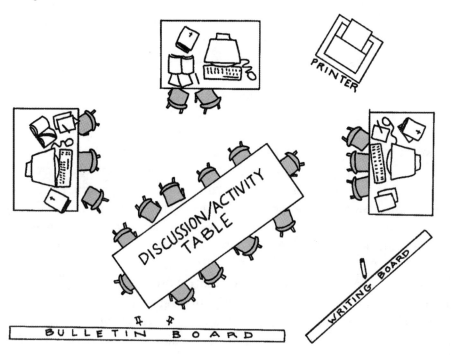

Computers at the Perimeter

OUTFITTING, LIGHTING, AND DECORATING YOUR LAB

As noted above, classroom tables covered with colorful cloths will work better than computer furniture for your workstations. Like any classroom, your computer lab will need Bibles, paper, and pencils. Have a set of Bible maps and a couple of reference works available for teacher and learner use. Your teachers will need a writing board. Do not use chalk and erasers on a chalkboard; the dust will accumulate on the monitor screens and in the computers. Use marker boards or chart paper and markers.

Use a bulletin board for special information to share with families and visitors to the lab. Create a "what we did today" area so that parents coming in at the end of the lesson will know what program their child used that day. This is particularly important since parents always seem to arrive when the kids have moved on from the lesson to more playful programs.

Have a clipboard or spot on the bulletin board with a sheet of paper and a pencil on a string. Have your teachers use this area to record "things to fix" for your techies to see when they stop by. Post a schedule that tells students and parents what you're doing in the lab that week and in the future.

Depending on the size of your room, ceiling height, and type of lighting, you may want to adjust or replace the lighting in your room. Low overhead fluorescent lights can cause quite a bit of glare on the screens. A warmly lit room with workstation lighting can create a wonderful atmosphere, help learners relax, and improve focus. Desk lamps that have a flexible neck work great.

Avoid Chalk Dust Near Your Computers

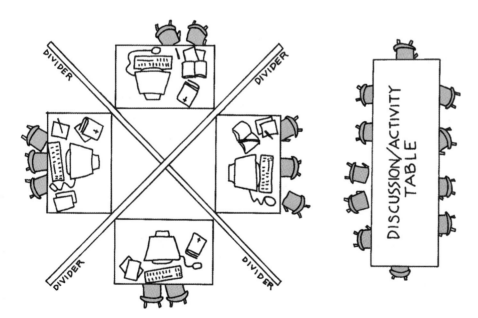

Computers in a Pod Arrangement

Classroom decor should reflect our love and welcome for our learners. Good teachers know the value of maps, murals, charts, and pictures on their walls. These teach in subtle ways, stimulate the senses, and create a warm, inviting atmosphere. Your lab doesn't have to look cold or sterile.

The walls should have information posted on them that learners can absorb in their looking around moments. Churches teaching with computers are coming up with some very creative schemes. Many use the colorful software boxes themselves to decorate the walls. The boxes will also inform parents and visitors of the depth and breadth of software in use. In my church, we painted scenes of how people have heard the Word of God through the ages, including scrolls, Bibles, and the computer.

Find creative people in your church to help you decorate with old or broken computer equipment. Keyboards, opened hard drives, motherboards, mice, and sound cards can be mounted on the walls or hung from the ceiling. The shiny disks inside the hard plastic diskettes or discarded CDs make great mobiles. You can even construct fanciful creatures from computer parts. The kids love it.

Create a Creature from Old Computer Parts

Wiring

Wherever you put your computers, you'll need to make sure there are sufficient electrical outlets. Make sure your outlets are all three-prong and grounded. Check to make sure the janitor or volunteer electrician from long ago hooked up the ground wire inside the wall box.

Use surge protectors with all your outlets. Lightning strikes can wreck havoc with computers. The surge protector's single switch makes it easy to turn off extra equipment with one flick once the computer is properly shut down. Unfortunately, surge protectors also make it easy to turn off equipment without shutting it down correctly. Be sure your teachers, assistants, and learners understand the proper shutdown sequence for your equipment and software. (Ask your techie to demonstrate this during the first training session.)

If you will be exploring the Internet from your computer workstations, you need to check on the feasibility of installing a phone line in your proposed location. You need one standard phone connection for every modem you will be using.

Opening the Doors

Early on in your start-up stage, be prepared for kids to want to try everything right away. This may be fine for a while, but plan to carefully schedule your classes and lessons so that students use a variety of software in purposeful ways without tiring of it. Some kids will only want to play the games, and they'll whine when you try to teach with other types of software. Post a schedule to help put your students' minds at ease about when their turn with the game software will come.

Some programs seem more fun than others to groups of learners and your kids will quickly size up which ones they like. In my experience, once kids come to understand that they are using computers for education and not just for play, they settle in and start to enjoy themselves, even when taking the quizzes. "Play your favorite" days, and game time at the end of some class sessions is a way to honor their choices and favorites.

After your start-up, and regularly thereafter, get together with your lab teachers to share insights about their experiences with the programs. Do not assume they're doing all that can be done. Challenge your teaching team to try new approaches to software they have already used.

BUT I DON'T HAVE...

Are you facing getting started with just one computer or older computers? Don't have a special lab room? We all have to start somewhere. If you have one computer, that's one more than most. Remember these tips...

➢ Don't try to start with a really old and cranky computer. Have at least a 386 with a sound card. The kids won't enjoy a silent computer and bad graphics.

➢ Jazz up that old computer by designing a special spot for it (like the Kwiz Kave mentioned previously). Give it a name tag, a paint job, and a false fantastic front (like ears and a hat).

➢ If you're sharing a room, define the computer lab space with something visually special.

➢ Purchase *Journey to the Promised Land* so that you can use your one computer with a larger group of kids. *Bible Grand Slam* and *Wordy* can be used with groups too.

➢ Avoid using your one computer as a "teacher's tool," and having the kids sit back and watch. That's no fun and they *know* computers are for kids.

➢ Demonstrate interactive software to "the powers that be" using a borrowed computer. Help them catch a vision of "what could be."

In summary, start small but be prepared to grow. Make sure you have the teachers, lab assistants, techies, and software to support you past the initial experiment. Do not discount the spatial needs of your lab. It makes no sense to invest the time and effort only to have it scuttled by lack of space and planning.

> *After your start-up, and regularly thereafter, get together with your lab teachers to share insights about their experiences with the programs.*

Chapter 6

Creating Computer Lab Lessons

Teaching with computers definitely does not involve just turning them on and walking away. Your teachers will be right in there with the kids. In some respects, you will use software quite like you use videos, art, or drama—as a component in a lesson plan. To be sure, the software you will be using is full of content. The content is there not only to be consumed at the computer monitor, but also to be discussed, shared, and expressed.

Your learners' natural tendency will be to browse through the content, always eager to move on to see what is next. This is part of the blessing and curse of multimedia computer software. It's fun, interactive, and built to explore. Your teachers will be with them as guides, prompters, and helpers. Your lesson materials and lesson plans will guide them and hold them accountable for what they encounter in the software (thus slowing down the browsing effect). View every part of a program as a springboard for discussion. Find the pause buttons!

In some respects, you will use software quite like you use videos, art, or drama—as a component in a lesson plan.

CHRISTIAN SOFTWARE AND TEACHING MATERIALS

Most Christian software does not come with lesson materials. In fact, there is a trend in the industry away from any printed matter accompanying the CD. Most developers consider their software mainly as something for home use. With the help of this book and a little practice, an experienced teacher will be able to create lesson materials to accompany software without much hassle. The software does carry a lot of the load. Lesson materials won't need to be extensive. (Sunday School Software Ministries produces free teaching materials for several popular programs. Consult Appendix B for contact information.)

Getting kids to use a computer and getting them to learn with a computer are two different things. Look for ways to encourage the discipline of learning. Because learning is fun with a computer, you are already headed in the right direction. Having the right number of computers with good software will help.

Creating Lesson Outlines

Each session in the computer lab needs a lesson outline for teachers and learners to follow. Begin by identifying the key learning that the lesson will emphasize through all its activities. This key learning should coordinate with what is being taught in the rest of the curriculum. Make sure each plan includes large group discussion and project or activity times, in addition to time spent with software. And don't forget time for prayer.

Computers are multimedia tools, so learning in your lab is already a multi-sensory event. There is no reason why your lab time can't include other media as well. Plan for Bible passages to look up and read as well as discussion questions to present before, during, and after computer use. Make use of posters, maps, slides, or the occasional video clip. For example, before heading into *Bible Atlas*, you might have the students read a portion of the story of the Exodus from their Bibles, then show a short video clip about Moses. After using the *Bible Atlas* software, move into the *Life of Moses* CD.

In addition to the lesson plans and materials you and your teachers create, make and keep a list of teacher tips for each software program. Many of the CDs you'll be using have so many areas to explore you won't be able to remember them all. Write them down so you can refer to them in other lessons. Create a file or notebook of notes and tips for each program and leave it in the lab for future reference.

Sample Lab Lesson Outline

➢ 5 to 10 minutes: setting the stage. Introduce the topic and its connection with the learners' lives. Do this away from the computers.

➢ 20 to 30 minutes: computer time with assigned software. Provide worksheets if necessary. Teachers serve as the "guide by the side," discussing the task with groups of students at their workstations.

➢ 10 minutes: follow-up discussion or activities. Discuss the key learning and its life application, occasionally expressing this through an activity or project. Include time for prayer. Do this away from the computers.

➢ 10 minutes: time for kids to play their favorite Bible game.

Creating Software Lesson Materials

Create instructional materials necessary to guide students in the use of one or more programs during the lesson time. These guides can be on worksheet handouts or written on a whiteboard. They might include:

➢ where to go in the program (and where not to go)
➢ points to ponder and respond to (often in writing)
➢ questions to answer (often in writing)
➢ program highlights not to miss
➢ things to look for and to record
➢ things to do after the program ends

Sample Lesson

1. As students arrive in the lab, invite them to go to the board and write down everything about the Adam and Eve story that they can remember.

2. Begin with prayer, followed by discussion of what they did and didn't remember about the story. Ask them to summarize what they think the story of Adam and Eve is teaching. Refer to lesson materials from the regular Sunday school class for help with this step.

3. Ask for volunteers to read aloud Genesis 3:8-14 from their Bibles. Ask the group to think of times they have behaved like Adam and Eve when confronted with their own mistakes and sin.

4. Send learners to their computer stations to use *Kidworks Deluxe*. Ask them to rewrite the ending to the story of Adam and Eve as it might have been if Adam and Eve would have immediately asked God's forgiveness of their sins. Tell them to create no more than three illustrated pages. Encourage them individually as they are illustrating and typing their story endings. Have them take turns using the keyboard and mouse. One student can type while the other creates a pencil sketch of the page they want to illustrate.

5. After about 20 minutes, take the class as a group to each computer and have the learners at that station explain how they ended the story. Ask them why they think the story might have ended that way.

6. Print out student stories to take home.

7. Gather as a group away from the computers. Read aloud Genesis 3:20-24. Discuss how God cared for Adam and Eve, even in their punishment, and how God forgives and cares for us, even when we face the consequences of our sin. Ask the group to think of examples of how they can forgive and care for others. Close with prayer.

Creating Worksheets

Give kids a worksheet these days and you're likely to get them flown right back at you. Hand those same kids a worksheet that helps guide them through a software program and they are as happy as larks. It's the computer. It makes them happy and ready to go. I have made extensive use of worksheets to serve as guides through the software in the computer lab.

Worksheets perform four important functions.

1. They help guide students through software in a logical and productive way without sacrificing fun. Multimedia Bible software can be sprawling. The click of the mouse is alluring and the "grass is always greener" on the next screen. Worksheets help channel the excitement and reduce the inclination to wander.

2. Worksheets hold students accountable for content. Unless your teachers are right with the kids every step of the way, learners may be tempted to skip through some content or they may be distracted by a program's exciting features and miss something you want them to see.

3. Worksheets help organize what a student is learning and can provide important input. Well-written worksheet questions and comments can help students better understand the software as they are using it.

4. Worksheets facilitate discussion during and after the program is over. They become a record of the content encountered. They help each student to be able to contribute to class discussion. They can also go home with the students or be compiled into a student's project book.

Some programs are nearly unusable in a church computer lab without worksheets. The maps in *Bible Atlas* are great and the brief articles uncovered by clicking on locations are interesting. I've taught with this program for years, but don't know how I would have done it without worksheets in the form of scavenger hunts. By the way, this idea of creating scavenger hunt worksheets applies to quite a few other multimedia programs, including *A Walk in the Footsteps of Jesus, Pathways through Jerusalem,* and *Disciples' Diary.* These hunts hold kids accountable for dealing with content. You do want to be careful, however, not to dampen their spirit of exploration. I suggest that whoever writes the worksheets also get into the lab to try them out and see how they actually function.

Sample Worksheet

One of the reasons I recommend Parsons *Bible Atlas* over other computer atlases is that students can click on map locations and read pop-up information about that location. This feature enhances the feel of a hunt. Below are some sample questions for the Exodus map from *Bible Atlas.* The answers can be found by searching through the pop-up texts in the map and using certain other features of the program. Each of these questions would be discussed in a group report after the hunt.

➤ In which direction did the Israelites travel to get from Egypt to Israel? How far did they travel?

➤ What kind of terrain did the Israelites cross?

➤ What did Moses do when they stopped at Marah?

➤ What did God give to the Israelites to eat in the wilderness?

➤ Why do you think God let them wander so much?

➤ List all the ways God provided for the Israelites on their journey.

The worksheet might also contain instruction on how to use the program. When using a worksheet, include what the learners have discovered in the class discussion following their time at the computers. To complete the learning process, you might have the class create their own giant wall display of the *Bible Atlas* map, complete with information tags.

Using Combinations of Programs

As you acquire software and experience using it, think about ways you can use programs in combination with each other. For example, if studying a story from the life of Christ with older children and youth, start the class in *A Walk in the Footsteps of Jesus* to see and hear about the location as it looks today, then go into *Disciples' Diary* for more information. For studying the life of Paul, begin with *Bible Atlas* maps related to Paul and then move into the *Life of Paul* CD.

Sample Lesson with a Combination of Software

This is a simplified sample lesson plan on the topic of psalms of thanksgiving using *Quickverse, Kidworks,* and *Wordy.*

1. As the learners arrive, invite them to add words or pictures of things they are thankful for to a piece of chart paper labeled "We Give You Thanks, O Lord." If necessary, suggest categories, such as home, church, school, mission, gifts, or relationships. After all have contributed, ask students why they think it is

As you acquire software and experience using it, think about ways you can use programs in combination with each other.

important to give thanks to God. Introduce psalms of thanksgiving as songs in the Bible the Israelites used for giving thanks and that we still use today in our churches. Locate the Psalms in the Bible.

2. Go to the computers and conduct a concordance search in *Quickverse* looking for references on *thanks* or *thanksgiving*. Have each student write down four or five references from the psalms and note their favorite two or three.

3. Have each student then write a five-line, personal psalm of thanksgiving. Working in pairs on *Kidworks,* have learners combine their two personal psalms into one by typing them onto the screen. Have them take turns typing and illustrating up to three pages.

4. Toward the end of class time, have the entire class go and read each computer station's thanksgiving creation. Print them out and staple them into a booklet to take home.

5. Turn on *Wordy,* the scripture memory game, and have students practice memorizing one of their favorite verses from the Psalms that they located earlier in the session.

6. Close the class session with a prayer and a favorite song of thanks.

PLAN YOUR SOFTWARE USE

Long-Range Schedules

After a period of experimentation with a variety of programs, you'll want to create a long-range schedule (for the entire school year if possible) of software usage for each age group or class using your computer lab. As you do this, consult the scope and sequence of the curriculum used in your Sunday school or other education program, and think about how to connect the computer lab lessons with the rest of the education program. Keep in mind special things for seasons of the church year, too.

Sample Long-Range Schedule

September—Take review quizzes on last year's lessons. Play and discuss *Captain Bible.* Write memory verses into *Wordy.*

October—King David Unit: Younger kids use *Life of David* CD.

Older kids and youth use *Bible Atlas* and *Pathways through Jerusalem,* King David segment.

November—Older kids create their own questions about David and play *Journeys to the Promised Land* game with them. Younger kids study the Psalms in *Quickverse* and create their own thanksgiving psalms with *Kidworks.*

December—Younger kids use *Star Chasers* and take Christmas Quiz.

Older kids and youth use *A Walk in the Footsteps of Jesus* with worksheet guide to visit Nazareth and Bethlehem.

January—Use *Kidworks* to create "Mission Awareness" inserts for bulletins and newsletters. E-mail New Year's messages to missionaries.

> *Consult the scope and sequence of the curriculum used in your Sunday school or other education program, and think about how to connect the computer lab lessons with the rest of the education program.*

Time Issues

Schedule at least 20 minutes of each computer lab lesson plan for software use. Some programs may take even longer, especially if the kids are younger, the software is new to the kids and teachers, or you are using several programs instead of just one. Certain CD-ROM programs can take nearly 30 to 45 minutes to complete if the teacher is fostering discussion as kids work, pausing at certain spots to point things out, or having the students fill out a worksheet as they progress through a program. Some programs like *Disciples' Diary* will require several class periods to complete. Some software, however, is brief in presentation. With tutorial and quiz programs, you probably don't want to have the kids use them for more than about 20 minutes.

When planning computer lab lessons, also keep in mind the time that will be needed to teach learners how to use a specific software program. The quality of your students' use of a program ties directly to how much care and time you spend teaching them to use it. *Kidworks,* the creative writing and illustrating tool, is a good example of this.

One last comment about time. Many churches end their computer lab sessions by letting the kids play a Christian computer game. If you will be doing this regularly or occasionally, leave at least 10 minutes or the learners won't get very far and they'll leave frustrated. This may be a time to introduce those games that are more Bible theme and graphics than content to master. *Captain Bible* and *Super 3-D Noah's Ark* are two examples.

Scheduling Students into Your Lab

An important task for the computer lab leader is to create a schedule rotating different grades, groups, or individuals into the lab. This can be an exercise in totally satisfying no one! There are some real trade-offs to consider. If you plan for more time between visits by the same group, your software will have an extended life, but the learners will be more excitable and anxious when their time comes. If you plan for more frequent visits to the lab by each class, you'll need a greater variety of software, but you will have more disciplined and focused computer lab students.

Just about everyone who gets started with computers ends up looking for ways to increase their students' time in the lab. There are realistic limits, however, and they are different for every church. There are even churches that have two computer labs, one for the younger kids and one for the older!

One strategy that will help your students feel like they are getting more lab time is to schedule them into the computer lab for several weeks in a row. For example, fifth graders could have the lab for one month, followed by the fourth graders for a month, and so on. This approach allows classes to work on one or several pieces of software over a period of weeks, increasing their mastery of the program and steeping them in the content.

Another way to extend a group's time in the lab while, at the same time, bringing in another group is to have the older kids prepare a computer lab lesson for the younger ones and then become their tutors. This approach works especially well when junior high youth are combined with early readers (Kindergarten and Grade 1). It also allows use of software programs with the younger kids that may be difficult were they to use them without assistance.

Sample Rotation Schedules

A month's rotation schedule might look like this for the Sunday school hour:

First Sunday of the month—Grade 2
Second Sunday of the month—Grade 3
Third Sunday of the month—Grade 4
Fourth and fifth Sundays—Grades 5-6

Here's a schedule that gives more computer lab access to the older kids:

First and second Sundays—Grades 5-6
Third Sunday of the month—Grade 3
Fourth and fifth Sundays—Grade 4

VARIATIONS IN LESSON PLANNING

If you will be using your computers on a weekly basis with the same group (such as a midweek fellowship group), you will need quite a variety of software. Supplement computer time with other related learning activities, such as art projects, service projects, and drama. With kids who are in such a situation of regular attendance, consider creating a "certification" program that has them explore one program over a couple of weeks. At the end of that time give them an award or certificate.

Another way to extend a program's life expectancy in your computer lab is to have your regular lab class "play" with a piece of preschool software and come up with some teaching ideas. Then, schedule the preschoolers in at the end of class to work with the older learners. As a general rule, older children will use younger children's software and learn from it if they think they aren't doing it for themselves. And the sight of older students tutoring the little guys is one to behold. Try doing this regardless of your software availability and schedule.

Creating and Using Computer Quizzes

The ability to refresh learners' recall of previously taught material is one of the strengths of Christian education computing. Over the years you will create files with dozens of quizzes, tutorials, and question sets using many different tools. Find ways to involve the kids in this process. When they help make their own quiz materials, it's a home run. They create it, they learn it, they remember it, and they enjoy it.

I use three basic quiz tools: *Journey to the Promised Land* with *Launchpad*, *Sunday School Tutor*, and *Testmaker*. There are other tools, including Wordy, the scripture memory game; *Grand Slam Bible Baseball*; and *Hyperstudio*, a multimedia quiz-maker for more advanced users. Each of these tools has its own role

> *As a general rule, older children will use younger children's software and learn from it if they think they aren't doing it for themselves.*

and requires varying degrees of computer literacy. Over time they will give your lab quite a bit of variety for quiz-making.

How to Create Good Quiz Content

The challenging part of quiz-making is creating good content. Trivia is easy to create, but it has little educational value. Instead, I recommend you create series of questions that are related to each other and to the key learning point of the lesson. Carefully craft your questions and possible answers to make your students think through their responses, engage in discussion with each other, and gather information that may be useful for the next question. It is important to include questions that call for recall of content as well as those that call for analysis, synthesis, and deductive reasoning.

Write questions that lead your students through a subject. When you give possible answers, do it in such a way that your students must read and think. Some answers can also be a way to relieve stress. Use humor.

Quizzes aren't only for testing and improving recall. Good questions and answers can help learners explore new information.

Sample Quiz Questions

These five questions illustrate the grouping of questions around a subject and the introduction of new material.

Q1: The word "Bible" means "the book." How many books are there in "The Book"?
a. 66   b. 23   c. 111

Q2: The Bible has 66 books with 27 of them in the second section. This section's name can also be translated to mean "new covenant." What is another name for the "New Covenant"?
a. New Testament   b. Modern Bible   c. New and Improved Section

Q3: What does the word "Bible" mean?
a. Book   b. Covenant   c. Holy

Q4: How many books are there in the "Old Covenant" part of "The Book"?
a. 39   b. 23   c. 111

Q5: Who is the "New Covenant" mostly about?
a. Jesus   b. Moses   c. Paul

Quiz-Writing Tips

➤ Remember the reading level and knowledge of your quiz-takers.

➤ Strive to include a variety of types of questions—content recall, analyzing information, summarizing information, and expressing the learners' own opinions about situations and characters.

➤ Be careful that the number of possible answers does not confuse or bore the learners.

➤ Use humor to relieve stress in test-taking.

➤ If possible, use sound, illustrations, and animation to give your quizzes a fun feel.

➤ Include "hints" in your quizzes to help those who are stuck. Some programs even allow you to graphically display a "hint" box.

➤ Include scripture references to encourage kids to look up answers in their Bibles.

➤ Vary your quiz types with multiple choice, fill-in-the-blank, matching, and puzzles.

➤ Resist the temptation to write long or difficult quizzes.

➤ Resist the temptation to write trivia questions or quizzes that don't teach useful information.

➤ Use your grading and scoring options carefully. Grading students can be a motivational tool, but it is more important to acknowledge and affirm students' efforts in the process than to focus on scores or grades.

➤ Create many quizzes in one sitting. This will not only build up your stable of choices, it also is easier to create several quizzes while the quiz-making program's instructions are fresh in your mind.

Ways to Use Quizzes

Use quizzes judiciously. Develop the habit of taking key learning points from lessons and developing quizzes for review a month later and again about a year later. Create tutorials or quizzes on subjects you have identified as important to your student's faith development. These can include learning the Lord's Prayer, the Ten Commandments, the books of the New Testament, and so on.

Many churches give Bibles to third and fourth graders. Develop a group of learning-about-the-Bible computer lab lessons that includes quizzes. Track individual student progress using a wall chart or file folder.

Confirmation class content can frequently be developed as a quiz or tutorial. For maximum educational benefit (and fun), have your confirmands create computer quizzes for each other and future classes.

Quizzes can be an effective way of following up another software program's subject matter. For example, telling your students they are going to be quizzed after King David's Temple tour in *Pathways through Jerusalem* will motivate them to focus on the information more intently.

You can also have your kids create quizzes about themselves, their church, the mission projects your church supports, or any other subject. This can not only be fun, it can help them explore new areas of study.

Help your teachers learn to not give out answers, but to help students discover answers. Some teachers feel uncomfortable testing their students. Some may feel like their students aren't having enough fun. Inexperienced lab teachers can mistake student concentration for student boredom.

Let me emphasize again that quiz tools should be used to motivate and refresh, not reward and punish. Be sure that all teachers and lab assistants encourage and recognize a student's effort, not necessarily their achievement.

Computer Lab Teachers

Like every other teaching and learning activity, a successful experience in the computer lab depends as much on the quality of the teaching as on the quality of the materials.

TEACHING WITH COMPUTERS IS DIFFERENT

Teaching in a Christian education computer lab is different from teaching in a traditional Sunday school or confirmation classroom. Not difficult, just different. Because it is different, teachers need to discuss the implications of the differences, experience on-the-job training, and be active partners in evaluation.

The biggest difference teachers will experience is this: the computer lab lessons start with face-to-face group time, but very soon into the session the kids aren't looking at you or at each other—they're looking at a computer monitor. This will be different, and perhaps unsettling, to uninitiated teachers or teachers who like to be in the center of the action.

Another difference is the level of student enthusiasm. Computers get the adrenaline flowing. In fact, this enthusiasm is usually the computer lab teacher's first challenge. Fortunately, student enthusiasm settles into happiness over time. You'll be able to accomplish more once they realize the computers aren't going away and that they'll get another turn.

The mouse and keyboard make the teaching different, too. Imagine if all teachers had a mouse attached to them so that the kids could control what they did and said! Well, to a certain degree that's what a mouse and keyboard do, they control the content. This is both a blessing and a curse. Students can deal with information at their own pace. Sometimes, however, that pace is too quick. Fortunately, most multimedia programs come with a reverse and a pause button!

Another difference I've observed is that children and youth don't think of the computer primarily as a teaching tool. They think of it as a toy and can tend to approach it like one. This is part of computing's great attraction and challenge.

One of the other great challenges of teaching with computers is that each piece of software can be so different from the next. All videos, for example, are played in basically the same manner, and the presentation of the content of a video is exactly the same each time it is viewed. Not so with computer software. Each program has its own operating instructions, and the presentation of the content can appear in hundreds of different combinations depending on the whim of the learner. For example, I have been through the *Pathways through*

> *A successful experience in the computer lab depends as much on the quality of the teaching as on the quality of the software.*

Jerusalem program a hundred times or more—using it with classes, in demonstrations, and for personal enjoyment. Every time I see something new. Every time I have choices about where to go and what to do, read, see, and hear. The same is true with most good multimedia software.

Teaching with a tool that has so many possibilities of how the content will be presented requires teachers who are fast on their feet and comfortable with the serendipitous—the teachable moments that arrive unannounced. Some bystanders think this method is rather undisciplined. Some call it the Socratic method. Socrates once said "a teacher cannot teach until the student arrives." He was talking about teachable moments. When and where that teachable moment arrives is often unpredictable. The good teacher spots them, helps create them, and knows how to discuss them with kids. A relaxed "guide by the side" teacher will encounter many such moments with multimedia software.

Having described the challenge, let me also add that teaching with software is a lot of fun. When was the last time everybody in your class was eagerly anticipating the hour? The results are great. They learn, want to return, and they think you're cool.

RECRUITING TEACHERS

Everything you know about recruiting volunteers for your Christian education program applies to recruiting computer lab teachers as well. The following tips, however, are particularly important to consider when recruiting computer lab teachers.

➤ Find adults who will make your computer lab their sole teaching focus. Do not ask teachers to teach their regular class and then also teach their class in the computer lab. Let them come with their class and be assistants to the lab teachers. Computers and their software require special attention and preparation. Do not let untrained teachers come into your lab with their classes to experiment with the software.

➤ Choose adults who are not intimidated by computers. Teachers, though, don't have to be techies. Churches are having great success finding people who are not comfortable teaching in a more traditional classroom setting (especially men), but are thrilled to be asked to teach in the computer lab.

➤ Keep in mind that having fine computer skills does not necessarily make a person a good computer lab teacher. This is a teacher's medium. Remember that your team needs teachers, assistants, and techies. Match the skills of the person to the job.

➤ Look for teachers who are good at teaching "on the fly." Especially for the computer lab, you'll want persons who can work without a detailed plan, have their own ideas, who enjoy being close with the kids, are playful, and can spot teachable moments for important ideas. Look for Socrates.

➤ Invite teenagers to be lab assistants. Most youth are computer literate and enjoy helping younger kids. They are particularly helpful when you have a class of early readers. Younger children enjoy the attention of older children.

Choose teachers who love kids and aren't afraid of computers.

TRAINING

There is absolutely no substitute for experience. This is one of the reasons I recommend you start small and manage your early lab development with a small number of teachers who have the time to get the experience. Early on they should teach for several weeks in a row in order to get familiar with the software and hardware. This approach will also help them see how different age groups respond to certain pieces of software.

Even if you will be rotating different classes into your lab each week, keep the same lab teacher over a period of weeks so the teacher hones his or her skills and learns how to adapt software. Pair experienced teachers with new teachers for two weeks in a row before letting new teachers take over.

Each time a new program is introduced, set aside time to debrief your teachers. Help them to learn from their mistakes and pass on their successful strategies. Remember to keep a notebook of ideas, comments, and tips for each software program. Teaming also allows experienced teachers to pass on insights into particular programs and point out those students who need extra attention.

Inexperienced teachers tend to just let the kids run the computers without much guidance or commentary. This happens not only as the result of inexperience, but also the popular misconception that educational software will do all the teaching. Yes, training, debriefing, and pairing is extra work, but not for long. And the results will pay off.

Remember that the coordinator of the computer lab also needs to spend time working in the lab to better understand recruiting and software issues.

Preview and Prepare

Knowing how a program works and being familiar with its content is essential to teaching in the computer lab. This takes time. Stepping into a computer lab to teach with a piece of software isn't quite like turning on a VCR and passing out leaflets. Teachers need to sit down in advance and use the atlas, play the games, and take the quizzes before they can know how to create the lesson plans and any necessary worksheets.

Create Good Computing Habits

The kids will naturally want to jump on the computers first thing. Indeed, if the lab teacher is not there early, they may already be sitting at the workstations when the teacher comes in. Once they are at the workstations, it's difficult to pull them away. Start every lab session away from the computers.

Right from the start, discuss and post ground rules and expectations. This can be challenging, but the computer offers you tremendous leverage with your students. They want to use and succeed with these tools.

> *Knowing how a program works and being familiar with its content is essential to teaching in the computer lab.*

The Bible Computer Lab Commandments

I. You shall love your computer and take care of it.

II. You shall not click on foreign icons without asking.

III. You shall compute in the name of the Lord.

IV. Keep the Sabbath holy with a good attitude and a desire to learn God's Word.

V. Honor your teacher.

VI. You shall not kill another's enthusiasm for learning.

VII. You shall not look lustfully at another person's computer or program. You will get your turn.

VIII. You shall not take more than your share of computer time. Share.

IX. You shall be honest and open about what you think, believe, and contribute to discussion.

X. You shall not covet thy neighbor's computer chair or saved place in a game.

Encourage Cooperative Learning

Encourage cooperative behavior and learning through structure and by instruction. Make sure everyone gets a turn at the controls. When groups are using a piece of software, arrange the learners' chairs so that everyone can see and participate. When students are working together on a quiz program, remind them to consult with each other rather than letting one person take over. When one student is at the controls, give the lesson materials, pencil, and Bible to the other student(s) at that station. When playing a game, have the person not using the controls make the decisions about where and what to do.

With creative writing programs, have students take turns at typing and designing. One student can think about some text before typing it while his or her partner completes an illustration on screen.

When there is reading to be done, appoint the person not at the controls as the reader. Have partners make presentations to the rest of the class about something in the program.

Teach your students how to use a computer and how to care for one. This will help build a sense of ownership. Take the lid off the unit and have a techie take your kids on a tour. Let them help you with upgrades and installations.

Keep Track of Program Usage and Insights

Have your teachers keep a notebook in the lab to record ideas and comments specific to each program they use. You might consider weekly evaluation forms for the teachers to fill out during your first year. These will come in handy if you are not regularly teaching, but are involved in the lab's management. Combine these evaluations with your worksheets, handouts, lesson plans, and "talking points" to create records for future use.

Have your teachers keep a notebook in the lab to record ideas and comments specific to each program they use.

Program used:

Date: Teacher: Grade:

How we used it:

What I'd do the same next time:

What I'd do differently the next time:

Look for Ways to Reward Effort and Chart Progress

This can be a difficult thing to do without sending wrong signals about competition and the value of individuals. We should be rewarding good effort rather than actual achievement. Your teachers may not initially grasp this distinction if their experience comes from the secular school environment. Do not be afraid, however, to ask students to "do it again and do better."

All Work and No Play...

Recruit teachers who recognize the value of play in learning. If your potential recruit has no interest in using a joystick or making it to the second level of the Exodus game, perhaps he or she should think about joining the buildings and grounds committee instead! You need teachers who know it is all right to have fun in God's house.

Interpretation

Parents and other church members will be walking into your lab wide-eyed and wondering. Encourage your teachers to view this as an opportunity to discuss the purpose of the lab and what you are trying to achieve with certain pieces of software. Encourage them to sit down and explore. Post a "What We Did Today" board outside the door for all to see. Invariably, by the time parents arrive the kids have ended their more serious programs and moved on to a game. You don't want them to get the wrong impression, especially early on.

On occasion, take a computer to the fellowship hall for show and tell. Or invite an adult class to your lab to explore a program like *Pathways through Jerusalem* or *Giants of the Faith*. Create a pamphlet that describes your program goals, the software you are using, and the subjects you'll be covering in the lab. Include a schedule of lab use for different grades.

ABOUT TEACHING AND TRAINING YOUTH

In the past years, there haven't been more than a couple of good Christian education programs for teenagers. Fortunately, this is changing. However, the time many of us spent in the wilderness these past years turned out to be a blessing in disguise. Instead of teaching teens with computers, many of us began using teens as teachers and teaching assistants. It worked out great. We brought our teens in to help with the younger kids and called them "Bible Lab Buddies." Not only did we get their help, they learned from the software, too, and learned about servanthood. Teens need training like anyone else. They also find it helpful if you have a short list of instructions and suggested questions they can use.

Several churches are reporting extraordinary success creating Bible computer labs just for their young teens to use. One junior high youth class made a promise to attend their class if they could learn with computers! They even raised their own money for four computers and software. Other churches, however, have found that youth can be a real tough computer lab audience because of adolescent peer-to-peer issues. The good news is that when they become Bible lab buddies helping younger children, youth tend to drop their guard.

Part of the additional challenge of teaching teens with computers is that computers are their world. They can be very judgmental about Christian software, comparing it to the latest $3,000,000 mega-game that has been promoted with mass-marketing hype. *Disciples' Diary* and *Pathways through Jerusalem* will hold their own quite nicely in this age group. So will some of the do-it-yourself quiz-makers, tutorial authoring programs, and multimedia presentation tools.

One of the bright spots with this age group is the use of the Internet. The Net is a very hot medium in their world and churches are just now beginning to explore how to incorporate it into Christian education. At a recent seminar, the only two people in the entire room besides me who had ever created their own Web site were the two eighth graders in attendance!

Internet tools are amazingly easy to use and inexpensive. Encouraging youth to create Web sites based on their church activities and mission efforts is only one of a number of ideas people are trying. Read more about this and related ideas in Chapter 8.

CONCLUSION

Be ready ... You're going to have a great time and so will the kids.

Be cautious ... Start small no matter how much money you have.

Be prepared ... Pay attention to the hardware, software, and lesson planning needs discussed in this manual.

Be surprised ... But not for long. Many in the church have been waiting for innovation like this in Christian education. They'll be ready to help.

Be a blessing ... Share with others your successes as well as your mistakes.

Be open ... God has given us a wonderful opportunity to do evangelism using an exciting tool. As this medium unfolds before us, we will grow and learn new ways of using it.

Christian Education and the Internet

We need to go where our kids and youth are. We need to reach out to them in language they understand and recognize. The Internet is a hot language for youth and children today. They're surfing with their friends, at home and at school. Ask most youth and they will tell you that the Internet is cool. They'll also tell you how much they and their friends are surfing out there. Every day around four o'clock, Internet services are swamped as young people come home from school and go online. Many of us know this from the firsthand frustration of trying to get an Internet dial tone!

What's the fascination with the Internet? People are attracted not only by the Internet's content, but also by the experience of surfing itself. Part of the excitement is not quite knowing what you're going to find, and the thrill of having the world at your fingertips.

This excitement and sense of exploration isn't just limited to kids. Many adults, including pastors and church educators, find the Internet to be an exciting, informative, and entertaining tool. This has led many of them to start wondering what it could mean for Christian education.

Doris Anderson is wondering. She's the director of children's ministry in my home church. One Sunday she came up to me all excited. "Chuck and I just bought a WebTV unit for our television! I could get into this Internet thing. We could be doing this here at the church." This from a woman who six months ago had never worked a mouse!

INTERNET AND CHRISTIAN EDUCATION

Teachers, pastors, and youth leaders in the church are beginning to surf the Internet with their students. They are using the medium with their kids to find and create resources, connect with each other, explore a world of ideas, and start some great discussion.

What's Out There?

First-time surfers are amazed to find a virtually limitless ocean of information on any subject imaginable. The number of Christian sites is in the thousands and growing at an enormous pace. Almost every denominational office, church college, and seminary has its own Web site with all sorts of information, resources, and links to other sites to explore. Beyond the denominational sites, there are those created by individuals (both adults and youth) and

> *Almost every denominational office, church college, and seminary has its own Web site with all sorts of information, resources, and links to other sites to explore.*

ministries of all kinds. These sites can include Bible studies, theological commentary and societal issues, ongoing debates, magazines, poetry, teaching materials, personal spiritual experiences, and religious products of every sort. Mission sites abound with pictures and information from all over the globe. Many of the mission sites tell you how to get involved or stay in touch with missionaries via e-mail.

There are also all sorts of fringe religious sites that are great fodder for youth discussion. Ultra-conservative, way-out, new wave, you name it, it's out there and growing by leaps and bounds. Part of the attraction of this medium is how wild and diverse it is. Make sure you have plenty of supervision when using Internet in your youth classes. Be sure to take advantage of the opportunity to discuss what your church teaches and how this is the same or different from the sites you visit.

Where to Find It

The Web by nature is vast and decentralized. To begin your explorations, I suggest you go to your denomination's site and to Christian sites that are collections of links to other sites. Go to www.websidestory.com, for example, and you'll find a list of the top 1,000 religion sites and links to other collections of Web sites. You can also find places of interest by using the search engines such as www.Yahoo.com and www.Altavista.com. Type in what you're looking for and prepared to be amazed. Prepare to spend some time searching for exactly what you want. The more concise your search technique, the better your results. Learning how to search is as important as what you are surfing for and will cut your search time dramatically.

The Internet is truly an opportunity to connect with Christians everywhere. Sites come and go, and that's why I'm not including an exhaustive list of Web site addresses. It is best to start with the larger sites and Internet search engines.

Christian Chat

Christian chat sites are also growing in number. A chat room is a location on the Internet where people are participating in an onscreen discussion by using their keyboards. People can respond to what someone has typed by typing their own message, and so the discussion continues. This is called a "real time" or "virtual" discussion. Some of these sites are for youth only. Your youth are into "chat" and there are sites that can be pretty unsavory. By exploring their world with them, engaging them in a discussion of values, and showing them Christian alternatives, you are doing them a service. In fact, the whole idea of confronting the temptations that anonymity on the Internet can create is an important discussion whether you're using the Internet with them or not.

Christian Rock

Do your kids know about Christian rock music? I'll almost guarantee you they've been to the MTV Web site! It's one of the most popular on the Internet. But there are a surprising number of Christian rock band sites complete with

> *Make sure you have plenty of supervision when using Internet in your youth classes.*

audio clips, videos, and testimonials. How could you resist a site titled "Jesus Freak Hide Out" or "Fish TV"? Along the same lines, there are a growing number of Christian radio stations broadcasting on the Web. That's right, broadcasting. The Web can carry music in real time and those providing it are producing some creative programs as well.

Visiting Non-Christian Web Sites

Teachers and youth leaders are not limiting themselves only to Christian Web sites. One youth leader was surfing the Net with his senior high youth group the week after the mass suicide by 39 members of the Heaven's Gate cult. They went to the cult's well-publicized Web site to view the cult's half-truth theology and wild claims about UFOs and comets. Four of his youth volunteered that they had already been to the site! That night, he said, was the best discussion about cults he had ever been a part of in two decades of youth ministry.

Those with a youth ministry background will recognize the teaching technique I like to call "The X Files—Ripley's Believe It or Not" method. Young people, especially junior high youth, are attracted to the weird, mysterious, and macabre. No wonder then that they are so attracted to the Internet! There are certainly plenty of strange sites good teachers can use to spark interest and discussion. What kind of world has God created? What is God doing in the world? What is the nature of evil and good? Visit Christian sites on these topics for sure, but why not really spark your youth's interest by also sprinkling in sites with names like The Abyss of Infinite Darkness, Millennium, and Frightful Things to Come? I know these sound scary and you do need to be careful. Do not leave their side if you are visiting Web sites like this. But also realize that your kids are already hitting these sites. They are also reading, going to movies on these subjects, and talking with friends. Some of the strangest or most controversial sites can provoke the best conversation about vital issues of faith and faithful living. Do all you can to encourage these conversations.

How to Surf with Your Kids

At the risk of sounding like a broken record (or a scratched CD), create an experiment. Put together an Internet hookup or bring your group to where one exists. Decide on a topic, and take them to a search engine or site listed above and see what they can find. Or preview a couple of sites and take your group there.

This first experience will probably teach you a number of things. The first thing you'll learn is that surfing draws a crowd. The second thing will be that the mouse is both a blessing and a curse. Getting them to slow down long enough to read is a task. They don't call it "browsing" for nothing. The Internet is built for browsing until you end up where you want to be. One hyperlink (a button to click on that takes you immediately to another Web site) leads to another, allowing the user to ultimately zero in on a Web site that is of most interest.

Once you are at the place you (or they) want to be, teachers are finding that the best way to approach the content is to encourage students to react to it, to

Confronting the temptations that anonymity on the Internet can create is an important discussion whether you're using the Internet or not.

wrestle with it in light of what they know about God, their own opinions, and yours. In this way, the content becomes a discussion starter, a place from which to spring into conversation. Sites that are a bit controversial usually attract the most interest and biggest reaction. This method of teaching youth has quite a bit of history and authority. I call it the "You have heard it said, but now I say to you" method.

Creating Your Own Web Sites

Many churches and youth groups are putting up their own Web sites. The content ranges from bland "what time we meet" to "come listen and look at our most recent mission trip." The best of these sites can help your youth see how other young people are expressing their faith.

You'll probably find that several of your kids and adults already know how to create Web sites. It's surprisingly easy to put together a site and upload it to your Web address. It's also a wonderfully reflective process for students to create sites about their spiritual lives, lessons learned, church activities, and opinions. This is a time-honored approach to teaching that uses new and exciting tools to accomplish its objectives. Do not post student last names or any information such as addresses or phone numbers on your Web site. There are some who surf the Internet whose intentions are not trustworthy. Be careful.

Many confirmation programs have their students create and publicly read a statement of faith. It would be very creative and inspiring to see these at your church's Web site. I'll bet the other youth in your church would be eager to see what their peers are saying! Parents and other members might too. And what a neat place for youth groups from other churches to surf. Through these kinds of activities, perhaps a little bit of Internet cool can rub off on the idea that it's cool to be a follower of Jesus.

E-MAIL AS A TOOL FOR MINISTRY

Pastors, teachers, committee members, and youth leaders are using e-mail to keep in touch with parishioners in an immediate, informative, and intimate way. A number of churches have begun e-mail ministries to their members. It is a new way to communicate with your members, extended family, and friends. It will help those of you who need Internet experience to get it. It can also put you in direct contact with resource people around the country.

Going to college these days often means getting an e-mail address. I keep in regular touch with college-bound members of my youth groups via e-mail. For example, Justin is a junior at USC. He sends me e-mail about his studies and life. I tell him about my life and what some of our mutual youth group friends are up to. This tool should end all our complaining about losing touch with our college students. Are you using it? Is $20 a month in access fees too much to spend on college ministry? What do you think that letter-writing maniac Paul would say to us?

> *Do not post student last names or any information such as addresses or phone numbers on your Web site.*

THE FUTURE

Few things are expanding as fast or receiving as much attention in our culture as the Internet. We are only a few years away from having Internet access widely available through our living room televisions. Doris, my non-techie friend, is already there. New technologies available today are rapidly advancing the computer's role as a daily information station. Simply fill out a form online now and your computer will tell you the weather, news, and sports scores every time you turn on your computer or view your screen saver. Imagine, for example, how someday we will apply this particular Internet technology in the church. Imagine being able to type a message into your computer about an upcoming special worship service or youth group meeting and having that information appear on your church members' televisions and computer screens that afternoon! In one sense, we can do that in a limited way now through e-mail.

As this medium develops and becomes more a part of our daily experience, we should see more and more Christian education Web sites popping up. For the church, the Internet could become another expression of an honored ideal: community, the church as body of Christ, people sharing their resources and faith with each other. The potential to connect members, educators, and pastors is immense.

With the Internet, anybody with great ideas, curriculum, and how-to manuals can be instantly accessible to anyone in the world. Sites are already being developed to collect such information or provide links to them. Got a great idea? Get it on the Web! This potential has been described by one Christian publisher as "the third rail for the publishing industry." This again will be a challenge as well as a blessing. It underscores the importance of knowing one's own theological convictions and how to use them in evaluating resources for use in Christian education programs.

We should soon see some Christian education sites duplicating the "long-distance learning" experiments that have been under way in public education. Dozens of universities and schools now have virtual classrooms and offer courses for credit on the Web. Students can interact with each other and the professor, and take online tests. The continuing education of Christian educators and pastors is another long-distance learning avenue to explore.

The capacity of the Internet to support real-time live video and audio is quickly becoming a reality. Imagine being able to join other youth groups and Sunday school classes in Internet conferences with compelling speakers. Imagine being able to link up for a live conversation with your favorite missionary in another part of the world. Imagine being able to broadcast your youth meeting or worship service over the Internet—spending less than $200 for the equipment. Imagine and then experiment. This revolution will be led by those who heed the call of the Spirit and step out beyond the familiar.

HOW TO GET HOOKED UP TO THE INTERNET

If you are not already hooked up to the Internet, you are going to be surprised how easy it is to do. It's as easy as 1-2-3.

1. Purchase a modem for your computer if it did not come with one installed at the factory. Plug it into the back of your machine and install the modem software. You can also get a modem that installs inside your computer. They start at around $100.

2. Following the instructions with your modem, plug your phone line into the modem. It doesn't have to be a dedicated line, any old direct line will do. If your church office has a special phone system you may need to find another line or have one installed. Check with your phone company.

3. Use your Internet software as directed to dial the local Internet access phone number you have subscribed to (if you have one in your area). Listen for the squeal of noises, and you're hooked up to the Net and ready to go exploring! There are many kinds of Internet software; *Netscape Navigator* and *Microsoft Explorer* are two popular ones.

Many places around the country have what are called local Internet service providers (ISP). These are companies that, for a monthly fee, provide you with a doorway to the Internet. Fees range between $20 and $30 a month for unlimited usage. You pay no long-distance charges for using the Internet because you are making a local phone call to your provider. Your provider is hooked up to the Internet's World Wide Web of computers. Many of these providers will also supply you with the software to navigate the Internet, such as *Netscape Navigator*. These programs are very easy to use. The typical account also comes with several megabytes of free space on the ISP's computer to keep a Web site you create for others to access.

Another option for Internet access is to sign up for an online service such as America Online, Prodigy, Microsoftnet, or CompuServe. These let you browse their own content areas or go out on the Internet. They have a number of other interesting features. Rates for these services vary.

When you are using the phone line to access the Net, no other calls can come in on that line. If you don't have an available phone line, consider using a fax line that isn't always in use.

Still not sure what you're doing? Don't worry, it's new to everyone the first time. Go find someone to help you—maybe a teenager!

Stories from the Front

Many educators have shared their anxieties with me about getting started with Christian education computer labs. I remember the feeling well. Teaching with computers is new and challenging. Nobody wants to fail, especially with something on which they've spent church money. On the theory that there is safety in numbers, I want to share with you some of the things people have shared with me. Here are a few brief stories to inspire your own.

From Nashville, Tennessee

I must confess that when I first visited Neil's church I thought computers would never work in my program. I was computer illiterate. We had a shared space facility and no room for a lab. And I had no clue how to fit the software into our curriculum. In the midst of these questions, however, a new pastor arrived in our church and he turned out to be a computer buff who was very encouraging about using technology in our program. So off I went again to Neil's church, this time with the chair of my Christian education committee. Her enthusiasm and support helped dispel my trepidation and soon we had the church's support and approval. A former storage room became our new lab and we opened during our Wednesday evening program. It was a hit and we now have plans to expand our lab.

It is rather ironic that this once "computer illiterate" is now called upon by other churches seeking information and help in starting their own computer explorations. One of the things I emphasize is thoroughly knowing your software before teaching with it. I also highly recommend that the regular class teachers who know their kids come in and help the lab teachers when the class is using the computers.

Shalom!

Carolyn T., Nashville

> *One of the things I emphasize is thoroughly knowing your software before teaching with it.*

From Bethel Springs, Tennessee

I am a 64-year-old, white-haired minister trying to help a small rural congregation do the things that attract the younger generation to the church. I have limited knowledge of computers. One day the word *presbyterian* kept appearing on the screen of the computer my son-in-law donated to our church. I didn't know it was the screen saver! As it turns out, this incident was a blessing in disguise. Angie, a young lady in our congregation, helped me solve the screen saver problem. I had discovered someone who knew quite a bit about computers.

Soon after that we completed a week of vacation Bible school using our computer and the *Life of Jesus* CD (New Kids Media). The biggest problem we had was getting the kids off the computer! Things worked so well that we soon were planning more time for the kids to use the computer. This tool is certainly a big help to Christian education.

Peace and grace to you.

Bob H., Bethel Springs, Tennessee

From Evansville, Indiana

We launched our computer lab with six kids, the church office computer, and a computer borrowed from a member. We began with *Star Chasers, Kidworks,* and *Journey to the Promised Land.* Each was a big hit. In addition, I've used *Pathways through Jerusalem* with my adult classes and will soon be surfing the Internet with my youth.

Needless to say, the kids are loving it. Our parents are, too. They are very pleased that their kids are excited about Sunday school again. Our results have been very positive and our plans for expansion have met no resistance. Our members are convinced that this is a positive step in the right direction.

Peace be with you.

Mitch P., Evansville, Indiana

From Golden Valley, Minnesota

I have always felt that computers would be a blessing. When I visited a local church already using them, I knew it. I did some reading and then took the idea to the leaders in my church. Surprisingly, everyone was gung ho.

We held a fund-raiser and received donations to buy three new computers to go with the three older ones we had been given. We found several teachers who were passionate about helping us get started. This became very important as our start-up was a big task, especially with six computers and the need for lesson plans for the lab.

How did it turn out? We are now in the process of replacing our older computers! The kids have been wonderful and parents have been very supportive. We found these things crucial to our development: getting to know the software before using it, developing lesson materials, and challenging our students to have some serious fun (and not just fun) with these tools.

Sincerely,

Ardys S., Golden Valley, Minnesota

More Stories and Insights

Kitty in Lakewood, Colorado, almost literally missed the bus on teaching with computers. She attended an educators' conference, only to find that the computer workshop she wanted to attend was full. A last-minute open seat on the bus out to the workshop site, however, became as she put it, "the beginning of something new and exciting. Frankly, our kids were shocked by the introduc-

> *We found these things crucial to our development: getting to know the software before using it, developing lesson materials, and challenging our students to have some serious fun (and not just fun) with these tools.*

tion of computers. Soon, so were we. They grew quite attentive, willing to learn, and happy to share. Our parents were impressed by our commitment to their children's education. Our computer lab drew a whole new group of people to help teach." Kitty's experience has spurred nearly a dozen other churches in the Denver area to start using computers in Christian education.

One of the popular misconceptions being dispelled about computers in Christian education is that they are beyond the means of the average Sunday school or small church. In the Dayton, Ohio area, a number of small- and medium-sized Presbyterian, Methodist, and Lutheran churches are using computers in their programs and have found hardware rather easy to get. Jo in Middletown, Ohio, was one of the first. "At first, we requested a computer only for the church library, and the trustees were less than enthusiastic. When we looked into using the computer in our Sunday school as well, the trustees approved the money without hesitation."

Tom's small, eastern Tennessee church didn't even own a computer until recently. Then one night Tom borrowed a computer, put some Christian education software on it and set it up at the church's potluck supper. "The kids didn't eat. They mobbed the computer. It was like a magnet. Our leadership decided at its next meeting that anything so powerfully attractive was worth exploring. A lot of our kids out here don't have computers, but that only made the decision easier to make."

Perhaps you could have predicted the use of computers in larger churches, but what about all these smaller churches? After talking with many of them, I've come to realize that the smaller church feels the slump of Sunday school attendance harder than a larger church. For them, attracting kids to Christian education programs isn't optional, it's a matter of evangelism and of the survival of the Christian community.

It is for all of us. Dub, from a large church in St. Louis, told fellow educators in his area that he was going to try a new model for Sunday school that included the use of computers. They were surprised. After all, his program was so big. Dub, however, knew the truth. "They were coming all right, but they didn't want to be there and they weren't remembering their lessons."

The growing experience with computers in Christian education is dispelling other myths as well, such as the myth that this is a young teacher's tool. Carol is a volunteer Christian education leader at a small church in western Ohio. Her kids began computing over a year ago in Sunday school. A number of her Bible Computer Lab teachers come from the retirement center next door to the church! Quite a few of the pastors and educators I work with are well on their way to retirement. For them, computers aren't about trying something new, but about the constant need to use tools that work.

In churches small and large, city and rural, the exploration with computers has begun. Some will no doubt say it's a fad. We tell them no, "It's only nine o'clock Sunday morning. A time for amazement and astonishment, a time for dreams and visions. Come see what it is all about."

One of the popular misconceptions being dispelled about computers in Christian education is that they are beyond the means of the average Sunday school or small church.

Chapter 10

Computer 101 for the Technologically Challenged

If you are bewildered—somewhat or a lot—about computers and some of the terminology found in this book, welcome to the majority. Only very few people really understand everything there is to understand about computers. We're all creatures of necessity. If you don't understand much about computers, it is probably because you haven't used one much. That's OK. It could also be because you haven't had any problems with the computer you use, in which case you have been lucky indeed. Most of us learn things about computers while trying to fix them.

I strongly recommend that you go to the library and check out a book about computers. There are several easy-to-understand books available for novices.

Before plunging into some "101" basics, let me put in one last plug for recruiting one or more computer-literate people from your congregation to help—a techie. Usually techies love to help.

The purpose of this chapter is to offer simplified descriptions of the basic things you need to know to be able to ask questions of your techies (and to understand their answers) and to begin to assess what the hardware needs will be for your church computer lab.

> *The purpose of this chapter is to offer simplified descriptions of the basic things you need to know to be able to ask questions of your techies.*

WHAT IS A COMPUTER?

The computer is simply a very dumb storage and retrieval device; it does what it is told. There are two primary information storage components to your computer. The main information storage area on the computer—the place where the programs that run the computer are installed—is called the *hard drive*. It is a round magnetic disk inside the computer and is usually referred to by the computer as the *C drive*. Hard drives come in different sizes, measured in megabytes and gigabytes. (A megabyte is a common measurement of memory space. It means 1,048,576 bytes—very small electronic pieces—of information. A gigabyte is one billion bytes of information.) Older computers usually have small-capacity hard drives in the 85 to 300 megabyte range. New computer hard drives come in the 1, 2, or 3 gigabytes size range. More hard drive memory makes it easier to store and use newer software.

A second storage and retrieval drive is called the *floppy drive*. It is called "floppy" because in the old days the disks that stored computer files outside the computer were actually floppy. Now the floppies are encased in 3.5" hard plastic cases. These stiff diskettes are inserted into the floppy drive. Go figure! The floppy drive is usually referred to by the computer as either the *A drive* or the *B drive*.

A relatively new kind of diskette for storing information outside the computer is called the *CD*, or *compact disk*. These shiny disks store 700 times more information than 3.5" diskettes. The CD is used by opening the tray of the *CD-ROM drive*, placing the CD on the tray, and sliding the tray back into the computer. The ROM in CD-ROM stands for "read-only memory." This means you can't change the information files on the CD. (Note: Some CDs and CD drives have been developed to allow the computer user to write new information on a CD, but this is off in the future for most computer users.) The speed at which the compact disk spins and sends information to the computer is measured as 2-speed, 4-speed, 8-speed, and so on. This is sometimes written as 2X, 4X ... The faster the CD spins, the faster the information gets to the computer screen. The CD drive is usually referred to by personal computers (not Macintosh) as the *D drive*.

MACINTOSH/OS, DOS, AND WINDOWS

Your computer comes with a master program that enables the various drives to communicate with each other to run the programs you want to see and hear. This master program is called the *operating system*. Macintosh has its own kind of operating system. Personal computers (PCs)—sometimes called "IBM-compatible"—use one of several different operating systems including: DOS, Windows 3.1, and Windows 95. Different operating systems require different amounts of *random access memory*—RAM—to run the program you want to see on the screen. Windows 3.1 needs 4 to 8 megabytes of RAM. A Macintosh system 7.0 and higher needs 16 megabytes of RAM. Windows 95 runs best on a computer with at least 16 megabytes of RAM.

When you are looking at software, it is essential to check the software manufacturer's recommendations on the box to determine which operating system can run the program. In general, older Christian software either runs in DOS or Windows, or both, but cannot run on a Macintosh unless your Macintosh has some fancy software to enable it to do so.

The latest CD-ROM based programs typically run on Windows 3.1, Windows 95, and Macintosh. This kind of software that works with more than one operating system is often called "hybrid." Sometimes you'll see the words Windows/Macintosh on the box announcing that it is a hybrid. Read carefully.

SO, WHAT IS RAM?

When you tell the computer to run a program, the operating system makes a copy of the necessary files and spreads them out to work on in a temporary storage and retrieval area. This temporary work area is called *random access memory*, or *RAM*. RAM is where the business of working with the features of the program happens. The more RAM you have, the more quickly you can do your work. A program that is trying to get sound, pictures, and text moving on the screen is working hard. The more RAM you have, the faster the program can process information. When you try to use less RAM than is called for by a program, it doesn't work out well. Some programs just won't run when there isn't enough RAM. Others, however, just work poorly or slowly.

RAM capacity is also measured in megabytes of information. Years ago, programs needed less than one RAM to do their business. Today, a computer needs to have at least 16 megabytes of RAM for newer programs that are expecting enough space to work their magic.

RAM can be added to some older computers. RAM is sold as little strips of chips that snap into *expansion slots* on the main circuit board inside your computer. This main board is pleasantly called the *motherboard*.

The computer monitor also has a RAM chip to store the video information coming up to the screen. This chip is on a circuit board or *video card* inside your computer. If you don't have enough RAM on your video card, the information can be bottlenecked on its way to the viewing area of the monitor.

PROCESSING CHIPS—THE COMPUTER BRAIN

Inside the computer, the RAM chip works together with another chip called the *main processor*. It is the computer brain where all information from a program is processed, or crunched. You probably have heard it called a Pentium chip or 486 chip. Older chips used to be numbered to tell them apart, thus: 286, 386, and 486. Macintosh numbered two of their processing chips 63080 and 64080. Lately, manufacturers refer to their chips by name: *Pentium, Cyrix, Pentium MMX.* Newer chips are built to be more efficient and powerful. They can handle a lot more information at the same time.

Megahertz

The processing chip uses electrical current to time its calculations and keep things in the correct order. So, a processing chip that can handle a faster electrical current can process program information more quickly. The measurement of this electrical current speed is called *megahertz (MHz)*. Some older processing chips ran at 16 MHz. Newer processing chips run at 150, 166, even 233 MHz and beyond. These higher speeds are necessary to process the video from new software. Read the requirements printed on the box of any software you are considering. This information will tell you how much RAM the program needs and how fast the processing chip should be in order for the program to run properly.

SOFTWARE REQUIREMENTS

Newer software programs tend to be much larger and more complex programs than those of the past. To store and process all this information and display it in a timely fashion, the balance of power among the various components is critical. This balance of elements is often called the computer *configuration*. Each software manufacturer recommends a configuration of computer elements for optimal use of the program. Carefully read these software recommendations before purchasing a program to run on your computer.

Most techies agree that software manufacturers tend to underestimate the computing power needed to run their programs. In other words, if they say 4 megabytes of RAM, it probably needs 8 megabytes! Experience will tell you if this is true for you as well.

Upgrades

You may get to a point where none of the software you want to run will work on the computer configuration you have. Upgrading computers is a possibility. This can mean adding more RAM, a new processor chip, a new video card, or a faster CD drive. Some upgrades, however, just aren't worth it. The rule of thumb is to not spend more than one-third the cost of a new computer in upgrades to an old one. At some point, the old dog won't hunt and needs to be retired. In general, however, upgrading is only a temporary solution. Newer software is stunning and future developments are likely to be even more spectacular. That's what we like to see, but it also means our computers need to keep pace.

Files, EXE, and Paths

If you are starting with older computers that have DOS or Windows 3.1 operating systems, you may have run into terms like file, EXE, and path. These refer to the computer's internal filing system. To use these computers, you will need to know about storing and retrieving files. Find a techie who knows these older systems to help you and your teachers learn the necessary commands to run software on your computers.

Monitors

It's a puzzle to me that some people will spend a lot of money on a computer and then put a cheap monitor on top of it. Not all monitors are created equal and, like everything else in the computer world, they too have evolved. Several years ago, the VGA monitor was most common. Now it's SuperVGA. The reason? SVGA gives better resolution (clearness) and better color. SVGA monitors have faster refresh rates, which means they can keep up to speed with the graphic output of newer software.

The monitor is connected to the back of your computer by an electrical cord, which is connected to a video card inside the computer. Many programs require a monitor and video card that can process at least 256 possible colors at the same time. The most common monitor sizes are 14", 15", and 17". Bigger monitors make sense if you're going to have several people viewing a monitor at the same time.

The monitor screen is made up of a collection of tiny, light-emitting *pixels*. The closer the pixels are together, and the more pixels per square inch you have, the better things will look. The size of the pixels is measured in *dot pitch*. A dot

> *Most techies agree that software manufacturers tend to underestimate the computing power needed to run their programs.*

pitch of .28 mm is better than .39 mm. The number of pixels across the screen and down the screen is written as 640 by 480 or 800 by 600. The higher these numbers, the more crisp-looking the graphics.

Sound Cards

Once upon a time computers didn't make much noise. Now you can play your favorite audio CDs on them. The *sound card* makes that possible. Sound cards are small panels covered with circuits and chips that snap into slots inside your computer. Most computers have a number of these snap-in slots so that you can add a modem, video card, and other neat stuff. Up until 1994, sound cards were 8-bit cards. The sound was equivalent to AM radio. Now the standard is a 16-bit card with stereo sound.

You may be able to add a sound card if your older computer doesn't have one. If you're using DOS software programs, and have an old 386 or 486 personal computer without a sound card, look around for an old 8-bit card at your computer store, repair center, or in catalogs. It will work fine. When your techie snaps in the sound card (per manual instructions), he or she will also need to install the accompanying software to run the sound card.

Speakers

Good speakers are important to have. Small speakers can sound tinny. Make sure you get speakers that have easy-to-reach volume controls. Headphone jacks aren't a bad idea either, except that your students won't be able to hear the teacher while wearing them! Most speakers come with built-in amplifiers to boost the sound.

Input Devices

A *keyboard, mouse, trackball,* and *joystick* are all *input devices.* The person using the software can use these to send information to the computer. Read the information on the software box to discover the input devices that will work the program you are considering. Some games can be played with either a joystick or a keyboard.

WHAT TO DO WHEN SOMETHING GOES WRONG

Programs lock up sometimes for no apparent reason. Sometimes it is because the computer processor just dropped a piece of information. Often, however, it is because the RAM memory isn't large enough or because students have hit too many keys or clicked the mouse too many times at once.

When a program locks up on a PC, give it a minute, then simultaneously press the CTRL, ALT, and DELETE buttons. This is also known as the "three-fingered salute." This will restart your computer in what is called a "warm boot." *Booting up* the computer is an old term that means starting it up. Be forewarned, however, that when rebooting, previous information from the program will not be saved (such as the file you created, the score you had attained).

To avoid potential glitches in programs, always close out a program and properly exit your operating system before turning off your computer. Some programs can become unstable over time if the computer power is turned off in the middle of them. Windows, especially, must be exited properly before turning off the power.

BACKUPS AND VIRUSES

Sometimes a hard drive crashes. Then what? Often, you end up buying a new hard drive and reloading all of your programs (fun), or you use the backup tape you made of your hard drive to reinstall your programs in one fell swoop. I highly recommend that you make a backup tape copy of your entire hard drive and put it in a safe place. If your hard drive ever crashes and becomes permanently damaged, you'll thank me for this bit of advice about getting a backup tape. A techie can help you make this backup tape.

You've probably heard about computer viruses but may be thinking you're not high-tech enough to get one. Wrong. Viruses happen. Anytime you bring a disk from another computer, you risk infecting yours with a potentially damaging hidden program—a virus. Viruses can wreck havoc in your system. Scan any diskette you are given with anti-virus software before loading it in your computer. In addition, run an anti-virus program on each computer about every four weeks.

Over the years I've avoided a lot of problems in my computer lab for two reasons: 1) We regularly give our hardware a check-up. 2) We've nurtured our student's sense of ownership and care for the computer equipment. Find a techie who can help maintain your system. Then write his or her name on your calendar as a reminder to call him or her every two months to do the maintenance.

CONCLUSION

Computers are like kids. They need time spent with them and lots of care. They're always outgrowing their "clothes" and every once in a while they crash at the least opportune time.

Computers are also neat tools. There are a number of excellent magazines for computer novices, including my favorite, *Smart Computing*. As you are learning, ask for help and training.

> *To avoid potential glitches in programs, always close out a program and properly exit your operating system before turning off your computer.*

Appendix A

SUMMARY OF START-UP RECOMMENDATIONS

This checklist is an outline of the start-up steps described in this book.

❒ After you have read this book, share it with two or three interested and enthusiastic people who are willing to make a commitment to be your pilot project leaders and with two or three techies who will make a commitment to setting up your hardware and software.

❒ Order and preview a couple of software programs. There are several recommended in this book.

❒ Demonstrate some of the software to your volunteer teachers and techies and to the decision-makers in your church.

❒ Put one or two computers, four to six kids, and your two pilot project teachers in a space of their own and let them experiment for a month.

❒ Share the results of the start-up pilot project and your goals and plans with your teachers, leaders, and decision-makers. Ask for their ideas and support before going further.

❒ Determine the number of computers you can start with, the location of the computer lab, and the schedule for its use. Create a reasonable start-up budget that includes hardware and software costs, plus necessary room modifications, such as additional outlets, tables, and door locks.

❒ Create an "Implementation Task Force" of two teachers and two techies who can help you get the hardware and software put together and serve as teachers and technical support crew for the first two or three months of your computer lab operation.

❒ Make an announcement to the congregation about your start-up plans. Keep it simple, saving the open house and other hoopla for later when your teachers are comfortable.

❒ Train teachers by previewing software together and discussing various approaches to using each program. Discuss how the software will complement the regular curriculum. Look for ways the computer lessons will connect with the scope and sequence of what the learners are studying. Write lesson plan outlines.

❒ After an initial period of two to three months, refine your plans and needs list. Solicit comments and suggestions from your teachers, lab students, and parents.

❒ Invite your education committee and church governing board to tour the lab and see it in action.

❒ Sit down with your teachers and techies on a regular basis. Continue to prepare teaching materials and preview new software.

❒ Recommended hardware for getting started: CD-capable multimedia computers with 16 megabytes of RAM, 150 MHz processor or higher, 8-speed CD drive or higher, 15" or 17" monitor.

❒ Suggested programs for getting started—Non-CD: *Journey to the Promised Land* with *Launchpad* editor, *Bible Builders, Wordy, Bible Atlas.* CD: *Pathways through Jerusalem, Kidworks Deluxe, Life of Jesus, Journey to the Promised Land* with *Launchpad* editor, *The Amazing Bible Expedition.*

Appendix B

LOCATING RESOURCES MENTIONED IN THIS BOOK

Note: You can find software by checking with your local Christian bookstore or denominational publisher. This list will help you contact software publishers, magazines, and ministries if you need help in locating their products.

Ark Multimedia 800-552-2807

Back to the Bible 800-759-6655

Baker Book House 616-676-9185

Bible Games Company 614-694-8042

Bridgestone Multimedia 800-523-0988

Chariot Victor 800-437-4337

Christian Macintosh Users Group magazine 805-726-2684

Church Bytes magazine 606-873-0550

Davidson Software 800-545-7677

The Learning Company 800-472-8777

Thomas Nelson Ministry Resources 800-933-9673 ext. 2039

Parsons Technology 800-833-3241

Rue Publishing 800-721-2439

Starborn Inc. 612-638-9300

Sunday School Software Ministries 800-678-1948

Tyndale House 800-323-9400

Wisdom Tree 800-772-4253

Zondervan 800-727-1309

Glossary of Computer Terms

CD-ROM Compact Disk—Read-Only Memory. More familiar to us as audio CDs, these silver disks carry far more information on them than their floppy disk predecessors. The CD drives that run them inside computers come in various speeds written as 4X, 8X, 12X, and so on.

DOS Microsoft's Disk Operating System, standard in most older personal computers.

Graphics Card or Video Card A circuit board inside the computer that controls the flow of video images to the monitor.

Hard Drive The main memory storage bank of the computer. The computer usually calls this the C drive. Hard drive sizes are measured in megabytes or gigabytes.

Internet, a.k.a. the World Wide Web Thousands of powerful computers hooked together via the phone lines across the world. Each computer holds files that can be opened and sent to your screen when you type in the correct address of the file you want. Local users of the Internet dial a phone number to connect to a local Internet computer.

Megabyte A common measurement of memory space. It means 1,048,576 bytes—very small electronic pieces—of information. A *gigabyte* is one billion bytes of information. More is better.

Modem The device that allows your computer to "talk" through the phone lines, allowing it to access the Internet and e-mail. The current standard speed is a 33,600 bauds per second (bps) modem. Speeds of 14,000 and 24,000 are also common. The newest modems are 56,600 bps.

Pentium The Intel Company brand name for its main line of processing chips.

RAM Random Access Memory. RAM is a set of memory chips installed in your computer, which provides an operating space for programs as they are brought up from the hard drive. Measured in megabytes.

Sound Card A circuit board inside the computer that allows the computer to generate sound through speakers. The capability of the sound card is measured as 8-bit or 16-bit, with 16-bit offering stereo sound.

VGA\SVGA Describes the type of monitor display. Super VGA offers sharper color and crisp-looking graphics.

Windows Microsoft's user-friendly operating system interface for DOS.